ARTHUR RIORDAN

Arthur Riordan's writing work includes *Hidden Charges*, and *MC Dev's Emergency Session* (both for Rough Magic); *Rap Eire*, co-written with Des Bishop for Bickerstaffe; *Love Me?!* (Corn Exchange's Car Show); and *The Last Temptation of Michael Flatley* (Macra na Feirme commission). As an actor, Arthur has performed extensively with companies such as Rough Magic, Druid, The Passion Machine, Project, Storytellers, Fishamble, and the Abbey and Peacock Theatres, as well as numerous film and TV appearances, including *Fair City*, *The Chosen*, *Borstal Boy*, *Bachelor's Walk*, *The Ambassador*, *The Last September*, *My Dinner With Oswald*, and *Joyce and Beckett Play Pitch and Putt*.

BELL HELICOPTER

A mutual friend introduced Conor Kelly (Dublin) and Sam Park (Bristol) in London, where they began working together in the late eighties. Armed with a four-track cassette machine, and a large box full of string, wind and percussion instruments bought from a retiring Russian music-shop owner in Swiss Cottage, they set to work. They started by recording music for friends' films, which led to commissions for film, TV, theatre and contemporary dance. In Ireland they are known for their commissioned work for CoisCéim Dance Theatre and Rough Magic, and they recently wrote and produced the score for the film *Hit & Run*. As a band they have performed live in various different forms at the Institute of Contemporary Art in London, Freunde Guter Musik Berlin and many other venues. Their music/sound design has been produced for the Royal Shakespeare Company, the Abbey, the Royal Court, the Traverse Theatre, BBC, Channel 4, RTÉ, Channel 5, Radio 3 and many independent films and projects. Bell Helicopter have two CDs on release: *Blade* and *Hit & Run* (soundtrack album), both of which are available through Small Fish Records.

IMPROBABLE FREQUENCY

A Musical Comedy

Book and Lyrics by
Arthur Riordan

Music by
Bell Helicopter

NICK HERN BOOKS
London
www.nickhernbooks.co.uk

A Nick Hern Book

Improbable Frequency first published in Great Britain
as a paperback original in 2005 by Nick Hern Books Limited,
14 Larden Road, London W3 7ST in association with
Rough Magic Theatre Company

Improbable Frequency book and lyrics copyright © 2005 Arthur
Riordan

Arthur Riordan has asserted his right to be identified
as the author of this work

Cover image: Alphabet Soup

Typeset by Country Setting, Kingsdown, Kent CT14 8ES
Printed and bound in Great Britain by Cox and Wyman Ltd,
Reading, Berks

A CIP catalogue record for this book is available from
the British Library

ISBN 1 85459 875 9

Improbable Frequency was first performed at the O'Reilly Theatre, Dublin, on 27 October 2004, and transferred to the Abbey Theatre, Dublin, on 4 March 2005. The cast, band, creative team and production team was as follows:

ERWIN SCHRÖDINGER/THE COLONEL	Declan Conlon
TRISTRAM FARADAY	Peter Hanly
MYLES na gCOPALEEN/MULDOON	Darragh Kelly
PHILOMENA O'SHEA	Lisa Lambe
JOHN BETJEMAN/O'DROMEDARY	Rory Nolan
AGENT GREEN	Cathy White

Members of the cast also played various minor roles.

Double Bass and Flute   Ellen Cranitch
Percussion   Robbie Harris
Guitar and Banjo   Des Moore
Cello   Diane O'Keeffe
Clarinet and Bass Clarinet   Conor Sheil
Keyboard, Trombone and Accordion   Cathal Synnott

Book and Lyrics   Arthur Riordan
Original Music   Bell Helicopter
Director   Lynne Parker
Set Designer   Alan Farquharson
Costume Designer   Kathy Strachan
Lighting Designer   Sinéad Mckenna
Sound Designers   Bell Helicopter
Musical Director   Cathal Synnott
Assistant Director   Tom Creed
Production Manager   Marie Breen
Technical Manager   Eoin McDonagh
Stage Director   Paula Tierney
Stage Manager   Aisling Mooney
Production Electrician   Joe Glasgow
Sound Engineer/ Sound Operator   Trevor Clinch

Set Construction   Theatre Production Services
Scenic Artist   Liz Barker
Projections   Tom Burnell
Sound Equipment Suppliers   Audio Services
Music Copyist   Des Moore
Graphic Design   Alphabet Soup
Publicist   Paul Fahy
Production Photographer   Ros Kavanagh
Administrator   Elizabeth Whyte
Producer   Loughlin Deegan

Rough Magic would like to thank Abhann Productions for the development and production finance that helped make *Improbable Frequency* possible.

IMPROBABLE FREQUENCY

To Carol, Aaron and Daisy

Characters

TRISTRAM FARADAY, *British spy*

THE COLONEL *of MI5*

MEEHAWL O'DROMEDARY, *radio presenter*

JOHN BETJEMAN, *English poet, spy*

MYLES na gCOPALEEN, *Irish civil servant, journalist and writer*

MULDOON, *IRA commandant*

AGENT GREEN/IRENE, *British spy*

PHILOMENA O'SHEA, *Myles's civil-service colleague*

ERWIN SCHRÖDINGER, *Austrian physicist, resident in Dublin*

STAFF *of MI5*

STAFF/SPIES *of British Embassy*

O'Dromedary's ASSISTANTS

Various PEOPLE *of Dublin*

A Note on the Dialogue

Improbable Frequency *uses a combination of sung dialogue and spoken dialogue, most of which is written in verse. In the original production, most of the spoken dialogue was underscored by music, particularly the dialogue spoken in verse. The sung dialogue is clearly indicated using the titles of the songs. Some of the songs incorporate dialogue spoken to music, and this is indicated where appropriate.*

However – what shall I say? –
Ridiculous.

Have a look at this.

He passes TRISTRAM *a loosely bound handful of papers.*

A wireless announcer in the Irish Free State,
Meehawl O'Dromedary,
Has come to our attention of late.
Primarily
By reading out requests
Which make mention of the Red Bank Restaurant,
Which we've long been aware
Is a well-known haunt
For Nazi sympathisers over there.

TRISTRAM *is leafing through the pages.*

TRISTRAM.
    Songs. These are titles of songs . . .

COLONEL.
    Correct.
    They're all from his programme, entitled, if you please,
    'Meehawl O'Dromedary's Moonlight Melodies'.

TRISTRAM.
    But why would you . . . wait! Yes, I see.
    Reference to the weather in the titles, could it be?

COLONEL.
    Well done, you're quick. Yes, quite a few.
    'A Fair Day in Dear Old Éireann',
    'You Make My Sky So Blue',
    'The Mist Across the Bay',
    'The Moonlight on Her Hair' –
    I mean, he might as well just say,
    'The White Cliffs of Dover
    Have minimal cloud cover
    So Gerry, send some bombers over there.'

TRISTRAM.
    And the titles really reflect
    The weather conditions, I presume?

COLONEL.
    What I'm now about to tell you
    Mustn't leave this room.
    The blighter seems to be

A master meteorologist.
The songs on this list we've made
Describe the weather
Not on the nights they were played,
But on the nights following.
A trickier prospect altogether.

I want you to go there, Faraday.
Find out what's going on.
None too glamorous, it's true,
But it needs to be done.
We thought of you.

TRISTRAM.
A field agent! Crikey! I flushed with pride,
Though I had assumed Éire was on our side.
Oh, I know they're independent, and neutral as such;
But really, aren't they British, pretty much?
The Colonel sighed.

COLONEL.
I'll be in touch.

The COLONEL *exits.*

Scene Two

We hear the voice of MEEHAWL O'DROMEDARY, *a radio announcer, making a broadcast from his studio at the national wireless station, 2RN, based in the GPO, Dublin.*

O'DROMEDARY (*recorded*).
Listeners, waiting, congregating,
In your homesteads everywhere,
Let my voice be permeating
The vibrating waves of air.
Let my words reach you safely
Through the gently crackling speaker,
And they not to be distorted
As they spread across the ether . . .

To all the decent peasantry
Across our gentle nation,
Gathered round your wireless sets
In rapt anticipation,
Whisht now, be quiet now,
A bit of silence please

For 'Meehawl O'Dromedary's
Moonlight Melodies'.

Parlour music begins to play.

TRISTRAM.
O'Dromedary:
Soon to be my tormentor,
This endless wellspring of pomposity,
And pettiness, and flatulent verbosity,
This . . . radio presenter.

Scene Three

Lights follow TRISTRAM *as he drifts amongst the restaurant
tables. Two of Dublin's old neon advertising signs become
visible: 'Why Go Bald?' and 'The Happy Ring House'.*

TRISTRAM.
Dublin.
And a sense of unreality
At once swept over me.
No, this can't be right.
So close to home, so strange to see
A city all lit up at night,
Lit up so flagrantly!

Members of the cast pass him by in a hurry.

Could these people strolling by
Actually be unaware
That something rather untoward
Is happening over there?
'The war' ring any bells? I see,
Well, carry on then, don't mind me.

My cover, by the way,
Is that the *Times* sent me out
To write up some articles
On life in the Free State.
That ought to justify my nosing about.
Or that's the plan at any rate.

A loud noise is heard.

A sudden commotion on the street,
Something nasty has occurred.
A young man sat in his car

And without a word,
Produced a penknife; began to slash
The instrument panel, every dial and gauge,
Till he'd hacked it to ribbons in apparent seething rage.
Passers-by asked him why
The sudden urge to gouge and gash?

A YOUNG MAN *is revealed at the lamp post.*

YOUNG MAN.
Obviously, I wanted to cut a dash.

TRISTRAM.
He seemed happy enough, if a bit confused.
I moved on, bemused, but it's his car –
He's made his choice, however bizarre.

O'DROMEDARY's *disembodied voice can be heard again.*

O'DROMEDARY (*recorded*).
Keep those dedications coming,
Every night the pile grows higher.
Dearest wishes go to Peggy,
Busy at the deep-fat fryer,
Murt and Michael, hardy men,
Fighting fit and strong and able,
Soon to meet in town again
To drink each other under the table.

Scene Four

Lights up on the bar, on top of which are lined, in tableau, the British OFFICE STAFF, *cocktails in hand.*

STAFF.
Ah, Mr Faraday!

Faraday?

The spy.

We're all spies.

We're diplomats!

Yes . . . (*Laughter.*)

Faraday. Hi.

Welcome to Mount Street.

TRISTRAM.

I called in to meet
Our diplomatic mission.
They cheerfully greeted me
With this admonition:

Song: **BE CAREFUL NOT TO PATRONISE THE IRISH.**

During the song the STAFF *and* TRISTRAM *perform a dance routine along the length of the bar and on various table tops around the room. The feel is very Noël Coward.*

STAFF.

Be careful not to patronise the Irish;
Good grief, you'll cry, that's hardly my intent,
Nevertheless, when he's inclined,
Paddy's mind is so designed,
He'll go and find offence where none was meant.

No matter how one tries to get along,
Unselfishly proclaiming Éire's undisputed charms,
A simple mention *en passant*
Of drinking, fighting and maudlin song –
Suddenly one is in the wrong
And Paddy's up in arms.

In Dublin, a young diplomat
Can realise all his wishes,
Provided he's not overly ambitious.
They speak the language after a fashion,
Haven't even begun to ration,
Try the beef, it really is delicious.
A spy, well, that must be a lark,
Cloak and dagger after dark,
Derring-do and gunplay, one suspects.

TRISTRAM.

Well, not in my particular line.
Cryptographers are more inclined
To leafing through impenetrable texts.

STAFF.

Well, be careful not to patronise the Irish;
They take umbrage at the kindliest advice.
Though it's clearly for his benefit,
Dear old Paddy's having none of it
When you tell him a little decorum might be nice –
It's happened to me, just once or twice.

I suppose they've had their woes
But all the whining, what's the point?
They could be British if they chose,
There's still that option, Heaven knows.
But mention that and Paddy's nose
Is further out of joint.

The searchlights converge on TRISTRAM, *isolated on a table top.*

TRISTRAM (*spoken*).
Is further out of joint,
Is further out of joint,
Is further out of Paddy's nose,
Be careful not to heaven knows,
Be careful not to parish woes,
Is further for the far the for
The force the far the rout the rout.

The searchlights swing away from TRISTRAM, *and the jollities resume.*

STAFF.
I couldn't help but notice, did you mutter something there,
As though you disagreed with my analysis perhaps?

TRISTRAM.
Not at all –

STAFF.
What was it then, a form of silent prayer?
Or symptoms of nervous collapse?

TRISTRAM.
Sorry, it's an occupational hazard, I'm afraid,
An involuntary reflex, a tic of the trade.
I hear a phrase and have to chase it down the rabbit hole,
Lips flip relentlessly beyond my control,
Freewheeling dumbly through word associations,
Slurred enunciations, absurd approximations,
Hurdy-gurdy slow rotations that spool and unwind
As the gears grip and grind in the treadmills of my mind,
Repetition, repetition, variation, repetition,
Patiently preparing for a spark of intuition,
Or hoping that a daisy chain of tenuous links
Will magically unravel the riddle of the Sphinx.
So yes, it's a prayer and a mental condition,
And a sign outside my brain that says: 'Gone Fishin'.'

But while I'm on my mission here I need hardly say,
I won't be doing anything to give the game away,
I'll blend right in, like you've evidently done,
I'll be ever so diplomatic and polite to everyone,
And though I may be horrified at how the country's run,
I'll be careful not to patronise the Irish.

STAFF (*sung*).
Yes, be careful not to patronise the Irish,
Though they don't object to patronising you.
Is it smugness or insurgency
That makes them say 'Emergency'?
I feel it lacks the urgency
Of World War Two.

Just remember dear old Blighty and the spirit of the Blitz,
And when Paddy's claim to nationhood is getting on your
    tits,
Just remember that we're Brits
And we're better than these shits,
But be careful not to patronise the –
Ah, bejapers and begorrah,
Careful not to patronise the –
Where the fuck is Glocca Morra?
Careful not to patronise –
Or otherwise antagonise,
Be careful not to patronise –
I'm doing it again, surprise, surprise!
Be careful not to patronise
The bloody Irish!

The STAFF *gather around* TRISTRAM.

STAFF (*spoken*).
Does he know about the other one?

Ah, the other one, now there's a thing!

We have another agent here, you see.
Splendid fellow, very bright,
Although he isn't really quite
The type you'd visualise a spy to be.

TRISTRAM.
Of course, the colonel filled me in.
You mean the poet Betjeman,
Your press attaché here, is that the case?

STAFF.

That's the one, you're spot on there,
You also ought to be aware
He drags a teddy bear about the place.

SPECIAL AGENT BETJEMAN *appears from behind the
bar, wielding a bowler hat and a cane. The* STAFF *go into a
music-hall routine.*

Song: **AGENT BETJEMAN.** *The* STAFF*'s verses are sung
while* BETJEMAN*'s are spoken in time with the music.*

STAFF.

MI5 said fetch a man,
But not some wretched tetchy man
For espionage can stretch a man,
But Betjeman – he just might do!
Betjeman – he just might do!

BETJEMAN.

Evening, Willis, evening, Lucy,
Welcome, Mr Faraday!
Just received a rather juicy
Letter from the IRA!

STAFF.

Letter from the IRA!

BETJEMAN.

They wanted to assassinate me
Till they read my lovely verse.
Now it seems they venerate me,
Tell me, Willis, which is worse?
Tell me, Willis, which is worse?

STAFF.

He's Betjeman, John Betjeman,
He's everybody's friend,
Most theatrical of agents
This side of the West End.

BETJEMAN.

Life's alarms and death's reverses
Seem immeasurably sweeter
Rendered into silly verses
In a silly, bouncy metre!

So with spies the same applies:
An operative is less alarming

If, despite his stealth and lies,
He's silly, bouncy, big and charming.

STAFF.
Betjeman, John Betjeman,
The natives think he's great,
Betjeman, John Betjeman,
Our man in the Free State.
Could Mother Nature etch a man,
Or Leonardo sketch a man
More affable than Betjeman,
His drinks are on the slate!

BETJEMAN.
Waft of Woodbine, pints of porter,
Pubs fill up and come alive.
Could I? Would I? Should I ought to
Send some names to MI5?

Far from flak, ack-ack and klaxons,
How I love these Georgian squares.
Soft the rain, and softer accents
Spill the beans all unawares.

ALL.
To Betjeman, John Betjeman,
Who else would have the guile?
Not some Turk or Chechnyan,
No, they'd stand out a mile.
But Betjeman, you bet'cha can
Rely on good old Betjeman.
Special agent Betjeman can do the job in style –
Can do the job in style!

WILLIS, *a member of the* STAFF, *has been tinkering with a*
military radio set. Now he's getting a signal. We hear a
stream of Morse code. The searchlights creep around the
room.

WILLIS (*spoken*).
Our friends again!

BETJEMAN.
Oh, Faraday –

WILLIS.
Transcribe it, shall I?

BETJEMAN.
Yes, please do.

WILLIS *types as the message continues.*

Been intercepting this stuff lately,
Should be meat and drink to you.

If you've time, of course. It's not
Your first concern, I know,
Even so –

TRISTRAM.
Yes, all right . . .

WILLIS *hands the transcript to* TRISTRAM.

I'll give the thing a go.
Who's the sender?

WILLIS.
No idea,
But it's coming from close by.

BETJEMAN.
Gobbledegook as usual.
Think you can crack it?

TRISTRAM.
Well, I'll try.

d, a, a, p, g, e, t, u, t, h, n, r, a, d, e,
i, i, n, y, o, b, s, t, s, e, u, f, m, e, g, c . . .

Good, we've lots of vowels here.

BETJEMAN.
You're pleased by that?

TRISTRAM.
Well, yes I am.
Likelihood is, all this is,
Is one enormous anagram.

BETJEMAN.
So we simply shuffle round
The characters presumably –

TRISTRAM.
Not with one as long as this:
There has to be a key.

Our agents use a poem code –

BETJEMAN.
Oh, is it one of those?

Well, you can do those bastards
With your eyes shut, I suppose?

TRISTRAM.
If I knew what piece of verse
They're using as a key.
Otherwise it's hours
Of trial and error, basically.

BETJEMAN.
Well, who knows? I'll leave it with you.
Now I've been told you want
To mingle with the worthies
In the Red Bank Restaurant.

So I've taken the liberty
Of setting up an interview.
Chap called Myles na gCopaleen,
A colourful cove,
He knows the scene,
He's in the civil service –
Local government, I think?

WILLIS.
A writer too, of some renown,
And quite the sharpest wit in town.

BETJEMAN.
But sadly, he's a demon for the drink.
I've read his book, *At Swim Two Birds*,
Don't ask me what it's all about –
The story somersaults and leaps
And winds up inside out.

WILLIS.
His column for *The Irish Times*
Now, that is quite unique.
Surreal, funny, tongue-in-cheek
Threaded with a vicious streak,
Inventiveness and wit aplenty
For the Dublin cognoscenti.

BETJEMAN.
Entertaining in its way,
But hardly all those things you say.
Oh, yes, he's ready with a quip,
And puns and bogus scholarship,
Elaborate absurdities

And multiple identities
And flights of fancy spiralling –
If you like that kind of thing.

WILLIS.
He wrote a book in Gaelic, too.

BETJEMAN.
Thank you, Willis, that will do.
The thing is, this contrary drunkard –
Gifted writer if you want –
Has recently begun to haunt
The Red Bank Restaurant.

We've had no reason to suspect
The fellow heretofore,
Still, you know, in desperate times
One never can be sure.
So meet him there,
Go gently, sound him out.
The landlord's name is Schubert.
I can recommend the trout.

As he speaks:

Scene Five

The Red Bank Restaurant. A waitress (AGENT GREEN) *in Berlin-cabaret costume is singing at the microphone on the dais.* TRISTRAM *enters and takes a seat.*

Song: **THE RED BANK RESTAURANT** – *Weimar-cabaret feel.*

GREEN.
There's a place where the barman will smile
If you drink yellow beer and you whisper *'Sieg Heil'* –
Not that we're Nazis, we just like the style,
Down at the Red Bank Restaurant.
Come on inside, find a corner and nestle,
You don't have to be blue-eyed or blonde,
Provided you sing a few bars of 'Horst Wessel'
Down at the Red Bank Restaurant.

Down at the Red Bank Restaurant,
Sing ho! For the schnapps and the linden tree,
Down at the Red Bank Restaurant,

And Ireland's opportunity –
Although we're not Nazis,
We're not bloody patsies
For Churchill and Roosevelt to tease and to taunt,
So we'll stick to our guns
And we'll drink to the Huns
At the Red Bank Restaurant.

There's a place you're sure to hear songs to
Let you know just who tomorrow belongs to
Down at the Red Bank Restaurant,
Down at the Red Bank Restaurant.
So come down to d'Olier Street and park up your bike
And whisper your dreams of a thousand-year Reich
Down at the Red Bank Restaurant,
Down at the Red Bank Restaurant.

Down at the Red Bank Restaurant,
If England's invaded should we really care?
Down at the Red Bank Restaurant,
These foreign disputes aren't our affair.
You may say the Aryans
Are only barbarians,
And you can shed tears for the Brits all you want,
But if that's how you see it,
Then you shouldn't be at
The Red Bank Restaurant.

The WAITRESS *approaches* TRISTRAM.

GREEN (*spoken*).
Good evening, will sir have a beer?

TRISTRAM.
What . . . Good God! What are you doing here?
Irene, is it you?

GREEN.
No, I'm sorry, my dear,
Keep quiet or we're dead, is that reasonably clear? –
Yes, the bratwurst is heavenly, try some of that –
Tristram, I'll meet you before very long;
There's an alley outside, we'll be able to chat,
For now, just be quiet or sing along.

(*Sung.*) Down at the Red Bank Restaurant,
Sing ho! For the schnapps and the linden tree,
Down at the Red Bank Restaurant,

And Ireland's opportunity –
Although we're not Nazis,
We're not bloody patsies
For Churchill and Roosevelt to tease and to taunt,
So we'll stick to our guns
And we'll drink to the Huns
At the Red Bank Restaurant.

We see MYLES na gCOPALEEN *at the bar.*

TRISTRAM (*spoken*).
What can this mean? Meeting Irene,
Here, of all places. Ah, is that na gCopaleen?
I won't approach him, not just yet,
I'll let him get his whistle wet
And see what I can glean.

Song: **MYLES'S SONG** – *a dolorous ballad.*

MYLES.
Barbed-wire *geansai*'d Nietzsches
Making speeches
Into their jars –
It's all my arse,
And furthermore,
Whatever whore
Pulled this pint
Is behind
The wrong kind of bars.

Can't a man have a drink and think
Of perplexing conundrums and bicycles stolen
And swollen footnotes in various styles –
Just file it all under 'too clever by Myles'.

Can't a man have a drink in this town
But some clown of the voluble sort
Starts to talk about 'ort',
And how the words of *At Swim Two Birds*
Are rather like Joyce's
Myriad voices –
Oh, God, can't a man have drink?

Can't a man have a drink without hearing them say
This isn't his first or his last one today,
Failing that can't a man have a drink anyway?
Oh, God, can't a man have a drink?

Sweet mother of God, can't a man have a drink?
And not have to think
Of weeping cows,
Murderous rows,
Priestly vows,
And the tiny, tiny screams
Of eternity trapped in a book?

And atoms colliding and running amok,
And bastard ventriloquists working in teams?
Can't a man have a drink though it certainly seems
Diversions have been taken to extremes.

BARMAN (*spoken*).
Keep it down there at the bar!
Tuning in, now, here we are.
Lovely signal, loud and clear,
Can everybody hear?

O'DROMEDARY's *voice can be heard again.*

O'DROMEDARY (*recorded*).
Now a dedication for the Red Bank clientele:
Philomena's ready, and bedad, she's looking well.
God speed, Philomena, you shall lie beside our foreign friend
That night when our long wait comes to an end.
Graceful, trim and ready for that special rendezvous –
Philomena, all our prayers go with you.
And we know that should our fortunes somehow be reversed,
Philomena will be ready for the worst,
Philomena will be ready for the worst.

ALL.
To Philomena!

TRISTRAM.
What on earth can that have meant?
And who could Philomena be?
Why these looks of grim intent?
I'll have to wait and see.
Better make my presence known
And get na gCopaleen alone.
All right then, let the interview begin,
Chin up, chest out, hold your noses, men,
We're going in.

He makes towards MYLES, *then stops in his tracks as he
sees* PHILOMENA O'SHEA *enter the restaurant.*

Whoa, back up, back up!
Who's this I see?
Standing in the doorway awkwardly –
Rather sweet and rather out of place,
Question marks and exclamations race across her face.
Is she really as sweet and naïve
As, clearly, she'd have us believe?
Wait, now, wait, she's looking at me,
Enigmatically.

Song: **THE INNER SPECIALNESS OF ME** *– light, jaunty, medium-paced ballad.*

PHILOMENA.
Lately I've been feeling like I'm going nowhere,
Just doing the same old rounds.
The Department of Local Government
Isn't nearly as exciting as it sounds.
Not for a girl who loves Continental novels,
Black coffee – any new experience –
And longs to be borne aloft on fiery wings of passion,
Though of course not in a smutty sense.

Then I saw him in the restaurant and looked into his eyes,
I knew straightaway he wasn't like the other guys;
He's got a soul that's sensitive enough to recognise
The inner specialness of me.

How much does he really know, and what's he going to do?
In any case, I've got my duty and I'll see it through.
Still, how might it be if I could only make him see
The inner specialness of me.

MYLES.
Philomena!

TRISTRAM (*aside*).
Philomena?

MYLES.
What the hell are you doing here?

PHILOMENA.
I could ask you the same.

MYLES.
I'm here to do an interview.
I told you that at work today.
Now what's your bloody game?

PHILOMENA.
  Oh, that's right, I remember!
  And what was the fella's name?

MYLES.
  I didn't say. Now go away.

  PHILOMENA *doesn't budge.* MYLES *relents.*

  All right. Stay if you want to stay.
  The fella's name is Faraday.
  He's been lurking there behind that table
  Ever since I came.

TRISTRAM.
  Oh. Excuse me, I –

  Together, MYLES *and* PHILOMENA *approach* TRISTRAM.

  Song: **WE'RE ALL IN THE GUTTER** *– a boozy, sing-along ballad.*

MYLES.
  So you're the smart boy from the paper?

TRISTRAM.
  Faraday.
  I was hoping you'd give me your views –
  A general impression of life around here,
  You can be as oblique as you choose.

PHILOMENA.
  Hello, pleased to meet you, I work with himself,
  My name's Philomena O'Shea.
  I just thought I'd say 'hi', and I'll try not to get in your way.

MYLES.
  Well, life in the Free State is rosy.

PHILOMENA.
  That's right.

MYLES.
  Surprisingly so, you might think;
  When the rest of the planet is pushed to perdition,
  And teetering there on the brink.
  There's a simple enough explanation,
  That doesn't take long to expound:
  We're all in the gutter,
  But some of us have an ear to the ground.

  It's a formula for all occasions,

But lately it's come to the fore,
There's not many folk can pull off the bold stroke
Of ignoring the Second World War.
So let's give ourselves a firm pat on the back
And keep passing the bottle around,
'Cause we're all in the gutter,
But some of us have an ear to the ground.

CHORUS.
We're all in the gutter,
We're all in the gutter,
We're all in the gutter,
But some of us have an ear to the ground.

MYLES.
Should we be supporting your forces,
As they struggle to keep us all free?
Well, horses for courses,
We've known those same forces
A little too intimately.
They taught us some valuable lessons,
What goes around has to come round.
Now we're all in the gutter,
But some of us have an ear to the ground.

Chorus.

PHILOMENA (*spoken*).
So Mr Faraday –

TRISTRAM.
Yes?

PHILOMENA.
Well . . .

TRISTRAM.
Philomena.

PHILOMENA.
Yes?

TRISTRAM.
Is that a popular name?

PHILOMENA.
Do . . . do you like it? Sorry, you're not quite what I expected.

TRISTRAM.
You were expecting me?

PHILOMENA.

No! I mean . . . you seem very . . . will you be in Dublin for long?

TRISTRAM.

Seem very what?

PHILOMENA.

I feel I can trust you somehow.

General shushing as the Red Bank Restaurant tune strikes up again, and GREEN *steps up to make an introduction.*

GREEN.

We've somebody special among us tonight:
An IRA hero who's fought the good fight.
His methods may gall you,
And even appal you,
So all the more reason to keep him at ease.
His name is Muldoon,
And he might sing a tune
So give us some *ciuineas* please . . .

As GREEN *passes* TRISTRAM, *she motions him outside.* MULDOON *in full IRA military regalia appears from behind the bar. He takes the microphone.*

Song: **TOORAL-AYE-AY FOR THE IRA** – *a rousing Republican ballad.*

MULDOON.

I'm a wild Irish boy; I'm the pride of my town,
In song and in story I'm widely renowned,
And if my roguish grin doesn't win you around,
Then I'll bury you where you won't ever be found.

CHORUS.

With a song and a smile and a *Sieg* and a *Heil*,
And a tooral-aye-ay for the IRA –
The Brits are at war so we'll give them what for
While they're looking the opposite way, boys,
While they're looking the opposite way.

MULDOON.

You remember that peeler who gave me that look
That I just couldn't brook, so by way of rebuke,
I brought him to book with me trusty slash-hook
That I took from me copious trousers,
That I took from me copious trousers.

CHORUS.
>   With a song and a smile and a *Sieg* and a *Heil*,
>   And a tooral-aye-ay for the IRA –
>   To hell with the Jews, just light up a fuse
>   While the British are looking away, boys,
>   While the British are looking away.

MULDOON.
>   Can anyone tell me, 'cause I don't know why it is,
>   Nowadays our intellectual diet is
>   Solely comprised of the cosiest pieties,
>   Hitler is evil? Oh, change the record.
>   We've heard it before, it's a boring cliché,
>   And we need to be bold in our thinking today.
>   But most of all we need to make hay
>   While the British are looking the opposite way.
>
>   It's time that we made the Brits understand
>   That we're taking a stand in our own native land.
>   They'll be feeling a swipe of the back of my hand,
>   And some Nazi torpedoes will do the job grand.

CHORUS.
>   With a song and a smile and a *Sieg* and a *Heil*,
>   And a tooral-aye-ay for the IRA –
>   The Brits are at war so we'll give them what for
>   While they're looking the opposite way, boys,
>   While they're looking the opposite way.

The habitués of the restaurant applaud as TRISTRAM
follows GREEN *out to the alley, the area by the lamp post.*
As TRISTRAM *leaves,* MYLES *picks up a plate with intent.*

Scene Six

Lights up on TRISTRAM *and* GREEN *in the alley outside. A*
FRANCISCAN FRIAR *runs past, clutching his smoking*
behind (this will be explained later).

TRISTRAM.
>   She waited outside for me,
>   Coolly amused at my amazement;
>   Led me to a shadowy recess
>   Where we began to reminisce.

Song: **THE CROSSWORD SOLVERS' LUNCH** –
spoken, over nostalgic, tinkling piano.

GREEN.
Remember where we met?

TRISTRAM.
How could I forget? Lunch at the Savoy in '38
An annual affair –

GREEN.
It was my first time there –

TRISTRAM.
The Crossword Solvers' Lunch was always great.

GREEN.
The Crossword Solvers' Lunch –

TRISTRAM.
The Crossword Solvers' Lunch –

GREEN.
We were such a clever bunch
At that Crossword Solvers' Lunch.

TRISTRAM.
The cream of cruciverbalists all gathered at one venue.

GREEN.
We had no trouble working out the menu.

TRISTRAM.
At the Crossword Solvers' Lunch
In the Savoy in London town –

GREEN.
You were the one across from me.

TRISTRAM.
So I was not too down.
We argued over imps and asps and ampersand and assegais,
And I wondered what the casual observer might surmise
As we toasted all the deities whose names are daily grist
To the cruciverbalist.

GREEN.
We toasted A, then A, Athena,
And old reliable Isis.
You said, 'Have we toasted Pan?'

TRISTRAM.
So the waiter brought some slices.
But you were my Venus,

Not a cross word between us.
I allowed myself another glass of punch.

GREEN.

At the Crossword Solvers' Lunch
In the Savoy, in London town.
You were the one across from me –

TRISTRAM.

So I was not too down.

GREEN.

And after lunch, I strolled with you,
The Strand, and Picadilly too.

TRISTRAM.

And each place name became a clue,
A powerful and magic clue –

GREEN.

Trembling on the brink of resolution as they sometimes do.
It may have been the punch, of course –

TRISTRAM.

My heart says it was something more –

BOTH.

As we walked together after lunch,
And just before the war.

The music segues into:

Song: **AGENT GREEN'S SONG** – *half spoken, half sung, over a jazzy, smouldering bass line.*

GREEN.

So what are you doing here? No, that's plain enough,
We're both at the Red Bank, why try to bluff?
You're a spy, so am I, so let's skip the guff,
We ought to join forces and pool our resources.

TRISTRAM.

This chap O'Dromedary –

GREEN.

'Moonlight Melodies'?
They've sent you to investigate him? Oh, please!
He's a loudmouth, an armchair rebel, it's true,
But couldn't they find anything more challenging for you?

TRISTRAM.

That request he played tonight?

GREEN.

> That was odd, I agree –
> 'Philomena', that's a new one on me.
> Could be some IRA floozy, I suppose.
> I'll ask around, see if anybody knows.

TRISTRAM.

> How long have you been here?

GREEN.

> Just over a year,
> Building up trust and serving up beer,
> Biding my time and minding my rear,
> Hiding behind this veneer.
>
> So good to meet an old friend –

TRISTRAM.

> Depend on me to the end –

GREEN.

> And there's no need to pretend –

TRISTRAM.

> Whatever lies round the bend –

GREEN.

> So good to meet an old
> Soul –
> Mate –
> Here –
> And to know you're near.
>
> Now, I'm Agent Green, I play mean and hard,
> No gloves, no quarter, no holds barred.
> When I mark your card, in the words of the bard,
> You're gonna be hoist on the joist of your own petard.
>
> Well, that's the idea, though I have to confess,
> I'm in fear of my life all the time, more or less.
> You'll have to tell Betjeman about me, I guess?

TRISTRAM.

> You'd prefer if I didn't?

GREEN.

> Well, frankly, yes.
>
> I've been getting quite close to Muldoon of late,
> And he's taking the bait, but the risk is still great.
> But suddenly he's boasting that he's got something planned,
> And talking about taking a stand.

TRISTRAM.
Irene – you're so – I mean – Agent Green!
This transformation, it's so unforeseen.

GREEN.
Tristram, believe me, it's just a smoke screen.

TRISTRAM.
How magnificent!

GREEN.
Just a routine.

So good to meet an old friend –

TRISTRAM.
Depend on me to the end –

GREEN.
When there's no need to pretend –

TRISTRAM.
Whatever lies round the bend –

GREEN.
So good to meet an old
Soul –
Mate –
Here –
And to know you're near.

I'm a Home Counties gal turned femme fatale,
I'm an English rose in exploding clothes,
I'm the bomb out of the blue; I'm the siren too,
I'm the heel of the oppressor in a Ferragamo shoe.

TRISTRAM.
I don't have to tell Betjeman, not right away.

GREEN.
Oh, Tristram, my sweetheart, what can I say?

GREEN *slides into the shadows, as* PHILOMENA *comes out into the alley, distraught, followed by an apologetic* MYLES. TRISTRAM *looks on in dismay.*

Song: **READY FOR THE WURST** *– Klezmer feel.*

MYLES.
Forgive me, Philomena, I just don't know what came over me,
Please tell me what to do to make it right.

PHILOMENA.

> Keep away, you bowsie, that behaviour was uncalled for,
> And it's obviously time I said goodnight.

MYLES.

> I swear to you, believe me, there was some mysterious
>   influence,
> Took hold of me and made me act that way,
> As though some outside agency had set up shop inside of me,
> And told me 'throw the food at Miss O'Shea'.

PHILOMENA.

> He pegged a schnitzel at me, and some sauerkraut as well,
> And strudels with a force you should have seen.

MYLES.

> I'm sorry about the schinken and that heavy pumpernickel.

PHILOMENA.

> The Germans make some dangerous cuisine.

> PHILOMENA *produces a large German sausage.*

> Next, he started swinging this, and aiming for my head
> But luckily I lunged and grabbed it first.
> 'Cause if I'd got a belt of it I'd probably be dead –

MYLES (*spoken*).

> As it happens, she was ready for the wurst.

> Philomena was ready for the wurst!
> My God! Did you hear that?
> Philomena was ready for the worst!
> It's strange, but suddenly I know,
> That for the last half-hour or so
> Every single thing I've done
> Has been a build-up to that pun!
> I heard a voice inside me,
> A tiny whisper first,
> But soon it was a bellow,
> And my head was fit to burst,
> Telling me to do it,
> So I took the food and threw it,
> As though I had been hypnotised or cursed,
> As though my body wasn't mine,
> Until I'd said the line:
> Philomena was ready for the worst.

PHILOMENA *and* MYLES (*sung*).
  There's something creepy happening here
  I feel it in the atmosphere –
  Everything is getting out of hand.
  Well, what confection does that swipe?
  What ensemble does it strike?
  It takes the biscuit and it beats the band.

MYLES (*spoken*).
  All that effort for a pun.
  Excuse me, now, I have to run.

  TRISTRAM *and* PHILOMENA *are left onstage. They regard each other a moment as the music rises.*

  Song: **BYE FOR NOW** – *very pretty, simple, circular melody.*

TRISTRAM (*spoken*).
  I should go.

PHILOMENA.
  Yes, I know.

TRISTRAM.
  Unless –

PHILOMENA.
  Oh, yes?

TRISTRAM.
  Was there something else?

PHILOMENA.
  No . . .

TRISTRAM.
  Then I'll go.

PHILOMENA.
  Right so.

TRISTRAM.
  Cheerio.

PHILOMENA.
  Cheerio.

  (*Sung.*) Bye for now,
  Or, ta-ra, should I say?
  Though maybe we'll meet again someday.

TRISTRAM.
Bye for now,
Or *slán*, I suppose,
Though maybe we'll meet again –

BOTH.
Who knows?

Who can say when,
Or where,
Or how?
So let's just say bye
Bye for now.

Bye for now.
It's been nice, I must say,
And maybe we'll meet again some day.

TRISTRAM (*spoken*).
Bye for now
I should go –

PHILOMENA.
I suppose.

TRISTRAM.
Though maybe we'll meet again –

BOTH.
Who knows?

(*Sung.*) Who can say when,
Or where,
Or how?
So let's just say bye
Bye for now.

They go their separate ways, leaving TRISTRAM *alone in the lamplight.*

Scene Seven

TRISTRAM *re-enters the restaurant, which is empty except for the barman who is completing a crossword puzzle in his newspaper.*

TRISTRAM.
The Red Bank was emptying out,
So plenty here to think about.

Myles was precious little use,
But Philomena, Philomena –
Strange that she was there at all,
She had no real excuse.
Said she felt she could trust me –
But with what?
Some mysterious plot?
I'd guess not.
But then that wireless dedication,
Well, tomorrow I visit the station.

First night . . . foreign city –
Well, not foreign, but . . . well, yes, foreign.
I'm bound to be off balance just a bit.
Going to take a little time to get the hang of it.
And how strange to meet Irene . . . Agent Green.
I used to be quite keen on her, you know.
She was up in London training at RADA,
Her favourite crossword puzzle?
The Observer. Torquemada.
We flirted for a while in a cryptic sort of way,
Then she drifted away.

He sits at the bar, orders a pint.

How much should I let Betjeman in on?
Mum on Green, that's clear.
I'll mention Philomena, yes,
Give him a general idea.

MYLES *emerges from the shadows. He regards* TRISTRAM.

MYLES.
Observe how the eyelids narrow,
In that puzzled, agonised
And deeply self-important squint,
As though he's almost cracked the thing,
You know, just need a teensy hint.

What's he after?
What does he know?
Has he executed that obscure fibrous attachment –
That is, has he cottoned on?
No, look at him –
In the battle of wits, he's an unarmed man.
I'll have to watch him though.

Scene Eight

O'DROMEDARY*'s voice on the air.*

O'DROMEDARY (*recorded*).
Good morning listeners,
Meehawl O'Dromedary here,
Summoned at short notice
To replace Prionsias de Paor.
Indisposed again, God love him,
Not the first time, to be fair,
But we all have our crosses to bear.
(*Muttered.*) Drunk on air.

My evening programme
Will be ably manned tonight
By Jerome J. Kelly,
So make your plans accordingly.
But now, gentle listeners,
Are ye ready? Are ye right?
We'll start the morning off
With ''Neath the Sunny Sky So Bright'.

We hear the beginning of a tune.

Scene Nine

Lights up on BETJEMAN *at a table in the British Office.*
TRISTRAM *enters.*

BETJEMAN.
Any progress with your mission?

TRISTRAM.
Bit too early to decide.
Na gCopaleen was ossified.
He had a woman at his side.

BETJEMAN.
A woman?

TRISTRAM.
No! Not in that way.
They met by chance, I heard them say.
You know a fellow called Muldoon?

BETJEMAN.
Isn't he the most delightful!

Hear he's planning something soon,
Something big and rather frightful.
But Irish women, aren't they charming?
So beguiling, so disarming,
And as is so often said,
They're bloody hard to get to bed.
One fellow seems to have the knack
Of herding them into the sack:
Schrödinger, the physicist,
Has charms the ladies can't resist.

Accordion music strikes up. We see SCHRÖDINGER *appear from beneath the bar. He's half-dressed, with a woman's stocking draped about his neck. He goes to the wireless set.*

SCHRÖDINGER.
Scheiße!

WOMAN (*from beneath the bar*).
Erwin, what is it?

SCHRÖDINGER.
I've missed O'Dromedary's programme. I must go over there.

He disappears beneath the bar again as the lights come back up on the British Office.

BETJEMAN.
The Irish leader, de Valera,
Brought the bleeder here to Éire,
To set up an Institute
Of Advanced Studies – what a hoot.
Dev, the prim and strait-laced prude,
Paragon of rectitude,
Seeks intellectual comfort from
The horniest man in Christendom.

Meet anyone else last night?

TRISTRAM.
Er . . . no.

BETJEMAN.
Very good, well, cheerio!

BETJEMAN *exits. The rhythm of the music changes.*

TRISTRAM.
Almost time now,
Not long to go.
Meet this fellow,

In his studio.
Almost time now,
Not long to go.
Yes, I'm nervous
Though it mustn't show.

TRISTRAM *is about to leave, as the music changes again*
(slow and sinister) and the other British Office STAFF
appear and make beckoning movements.

STAFF.
Faraday!

TRISTRAM.
What?

STAFF.
Faraday!

TRISTRAM.
Willis! Lucy!

STAFF.
If we may . . .

Making a great show of secrecy, they take him aside.

Song: **CERTAIN THINGS** – *eerie, foreboding feel, minor*
chords and an unsettling time signature.

STAFF.
There is something that you really ought to hear:
Certain things
Are occurring.
Unlovely
Forces
Are stirring here.

It's essential that we don't create a fuss.
Not a word,
Mustn't query
These things;
But it's eerie,
And serious.

A young man sat
In his car and
He began to slash
At the dials –
Said he wanted
To cut a dash.

A portly
Franciscan
Almost went on fire
Reading Hegel
On the cooker –
Said he's a deep fat friar.

Every incident revolves around a pun.
What madness
Have we here?
What solace
Do they find?
What kind of fun?

TRISTRAM.
    You must think I'm even greener than I seem.
    What a story!

STAFF.
    Please believe me!
    This is real,
    Though it feels like
    Some fevered dream.

    That case where
    Two men went
    On a ghastly spree –
    Drank each other
    Under the table
    Quite literally.

With a last, significant look, the STAFF *disperses and exits.*

Scene Ten

TRISTRAM.
    Now, that didn't make any sense!
    And yet . . . and yet . . .
    I'd seen some incidents.
    Last night's debacle with the wurst –
    And that first
    Encounter with the chap who slashed his car.
    Still, this unexpected turn
    Was hardly my concern.
    Far more important I should go
    To the fabled GPO,
    The home of Irish radio,

O'Dromedary's studio.
(Rather impressive portico.)

Well, well!
I'd stood there at the door
And there, before me,
Philomena –
It seems we meet once more.

Lights up on O'DROMEDARY *in his radio studio. He is in conversation with* PHILOMENA *as* TRISTRAM *enters.*

Scene Eleven

PHILOMENA.
    Play this tomorrow night, Meehawl?
    'How Clear the Sky Above'?
    I hate to bother you at all
    But that's a song I love.

O'DROMEDARY.
    You have me pestered, Miss O'Shea.
    Last week you asked for 'Bright As Day',
    Before that, it was, what was it?
    Oh, yes, 'The Mist Across the Bay'.

    They notice TRISTRAM. PHILOMENA *looks flustered.*

PHILOMENA.
    Tristram! Thanks, Meehawl, that's great.
    Fancy meeting you!

TRISTRAM.
    Yes, I'm calling round to do
    Another interview.

Song: **I'M ANTI-BRITISH, IT'S JUST MY WAY** –
cheery, flag-waving music-hall number.

O'DROMEDARY (*spoken*).
    Mr Faraday? Begob!
    I trust our country's to your liking?
    Then, it's always been a draw,
    To Anglo-Saxon, Norman, Viking.

    No hard feelings now, of course,
    A journalist? I see, I see,
    Excused from active service
    Through some disability?

TRISTRAM.
Well, no, that is –

O'DROMEDARY (*sung*).
Ah, don't mind me, I'm anti-British,
That's my way.
You have to make allowances,
And be careful what you say.

TRISTRAM (*spoken*).
I see. That's very forthright.
Could you say, at any rate,
Is the war a tricky subject
Here in the Free State?

O'DROMEDARY.
Oho! Don't start me! Censorship!
It's dismal altogether.
D'you know, I'm not allowed to broadcast
A word about the weather?

De Valera doesn't want
The Brits upset you see,
So we kow-tow as usual –
Is that neutrality?

(*Sung.*) Don't mind me, I'm anti-British,
Certified,
It's just your native prejudice
I simply can't abide.

O'DROMEDARY'*s* ASSISTANT *enters.*

ASSISTANT (*spoken*).
Sir, I've Dr Schrödinger outside.
I couldn't put him off no matter how I tried,
He wants to pick your brains again.

O'DROMEDARY.
Suppose I'd better see him, then.

PHILOMENA.
Oh, God, now there's a specimen
I really can't abide!

SCHRÖDINGER *enters.*

Song: **DON'T YOU WAVE YOUR PARTICLES AT ME** –
music-hall with an Alpine flavour.

SCHRÖDINGER.
I'm Erwin Schrödinger, that's right.

The Irish State extended me a kind invite
To work here at the Institute,
Sehr gut, the Fräuleins here are cute,
And I was hoping I might shoot
My load tonight.

I won the Nobel Prize in '33
For my work on sub-atomic theory.
Philomena, how are you?
You know what I want to do?

PHILOMENA.
If you know what's good for you,
You'll keep away from me.

O'DROMEDARY's ASSISTANTS *are drinking lager and
yodelling, as a Tyrolean chorus.*

SCHRÖDINGER.
Philomena, please!

ASSISTANT 1.
Yodell–eh–eh–ho.

SCHRÖDINGER.
I need the sweet release!

ASSISTANT 2.
Yodell–eh–eh–ho.

SCHRÖDINGER.
In my mind's eye all I see
Is particle and wave duality.

PHILOMENA.
Well, don't you wave your particles at me!
Don't you have a shred of human decency?

SCHRÖDINGER.
Heisenberg's uncertainty
Need not apply to you and me.
You find the right position
And I'll give it some velocity.

PHILOMENA.
Don't you wave your particles at me!
Erwin, must you keep this up so constantly?

SCHRÖDINGER.
Planck's constant, not like me,
Just give me some duality.

You ought to meet my secretaries,
Who knows, there might be chemistry!

ALL.
The pleasures of the mind
Are subtle and refined –

SCHRÖDINGER.
But come the evening all I want to do
Is be buried up to my back wheels in you.

PHILOMENA.
Don't you wave your particles at me!
There's certain things a lady really shouldn't see.
And you might think it's smart to kill
A cat, you dirty article,
But don't you wave your filthy particles at me!

SCHRÖDINGER.
Philomena, please!

ASSISTANT 1.
Yodell–eh–eh–ho.

SCHRÖDINGER.
I need the sweet release!

ASSISTANT 2.
Yodell–eh–eh–ho.

SCHRÖDINGER.
I like the pleasures of the mind,
But equally I treasure your behind.

ALL.
Equally he treasures –

SCHRÖDINGER.
Equally I treasure –

ALL.
Equally he treasure your behind.

O'DROMEDARY (*spoken*).
Herr Schrödinger, you're here again!
Begob, I'm in demand today.
Me man is from the London *Times*,
A Mr Faraday.

SCHRÖDINGER.
Faraday! I see . . . and Philomena
I already know.

PHILOMENA.
>Yes. Excuse me, gentlemen,
>I really ought to go.

>PHILOMENA *passes* TRISTRAM, *avoiding his look. She exits.*

SCHRÖDINGER.
>Meehawl, I missed your show this morning.
>Let me ask you if I may,
>Can you recall which rousing
>Compositions did you play?

O'DROMEDARY.
>Well, now, let me see,
>Oh, you don't really want to know . . .

SCHRÖDINGER.
>Please, if you would be so kind –

O'DROMEDARY.
>'Oft In Darkling Groves Entwined' –
>'The Little Darkey's Prayer' –
>'Me Jaunty Jarvey's Car' –

SCHRÖDINGER.
>Thank you, thank you, what a mind!

O'DROMEDARY.
>There's more –

SCHRÖDINGER.
>No, stop right there!
>Stop where you are.
>You have excelled yourself again.

O'DROMEDARY.
>So, Erwin tell me –

SCHRÖDINGER.
>Danke, I must go, auf Wiedersehen.

O'DROMEDARY.
>But your boys are the horse to back
>Right now, I'd have to say?

SCHRÖDINGER.
>Meehawl, I'm not a German.

O'DROMEDARY.
>Oh, right, *Austrian.* Fair play.
>And Erwin –

SCHRÖDINGER.
  Please, I must be off.

O'DROMEDARY.
  Fair enough, goodbye, goodbye.

  SCHRÖDINGER *exits.*

  Everyone is rushing off today,
  I wonder why?
  At least the waves are mild right now,
  Hardly palpable at all.
  Normally by now they'd have me
  Flattened to the wall.

TRISTRAM.
  I'm sorry?

O'DROMEDARY.
  Radio waves:
  They gather here, you see,
  Before they go outside
  To work their tricky ministry.

TRISTRAM.
  You're telling me you can feel . . . radio waves?

  Song: **THE WAVES, O THE WAVES** – *parlour ballad.*

  As O'DROMEDARY *sings, the room is suffused with
  ripples of light, an aurora borealis of radio frequencies.
  Two of* O'DROMEDARY'S ASSISTANTS *become a chorus
  of crooners.*

O'DROMEDARY.
  The waves, o the waves
  Vibrating everywhere,
  Around the Earth
  They leap invisibly.
  And as I speak,
  Their motion fills the air,
  And every molecule of you and me,
  And every molecule of you and me.

  Crystals and wires,
  Inanimate and senseless,
  Obey the waves
  And sing beneath their spell.
  If copper and stone
  Are rendered so defenceless,

Can human flesh be less susceptible?
Can human flesh be less susceptible?

You mark my words,
Their power is daily growing
And soon the waves
Will hold us in their thrall.
We humble slaves
Will do their will unknowing,
Will do their will, and answer to their call,
Will do their will, and answer to their call.

Scene Twelve

TRISTRAM *wanders out of the GPO.*

TRISTRAM.
O'Dromedary seemed insane,
That much was plain;
But then again,
Why had Schrödinger appeared?
Now that was weird.
Why had he wanted to know
What songs O'Dromedary had played
That morning on his show?
Obviously
Philomena's deep in this,
Whatever this might be.
She turns up everywhere I go;
She knows O'Dromedary,
And it seems she's requested
Several songs alluding to the weather.
So taken all together . . .

The light changes, brightening, opening out.

As I left the GPO,
This dowdy, grey,
Wet-blanket cloudy day
Peeled away
To reveal – I say!
Lazy amber sunbeams,
Bumble-bee golden haze,
And cheeky-postcard cobalt blue sky.
The Irish weather, it seems,

Is having one of its days.
Let's face it, so am I.
Clearly the best place by far
To spend a sun-kissed afternoon like this
Is in the dark recesses
Of the Palace Bar.

Scene Thirteen

TRISTRAM *enters the Palace Bar on Dublin's Fleet Street, where the local revellers are singing. As they sing, the barman venerates a chalice full of potato crisps and a pint of Guinness, raising them aloft as at communion.*

Song: **A HYMN TO DRINK** – *a slow ecclesiastical chant, but with a sudden rousing, rebellious chorus.*

ALL.
Sláinte agus saol,
May your powers never fail,
May you smile at the troubles you once cursed.
Leave your cares at the door,
We have gargle galore,
And the last drop as gentle as the first.

And when closing time is called may you be favoured with
a wink,
A sound and valued customer, you'll stay for one more drink.

Sláinte agus saol,
Sláinte agus saol,
Sláinte, sláinte agus saol.

When it's dark and it's damp,
And the chill gives you cramp,
And the rain has found a channel down your back,
Sit down here and wait
While you anticipate
A great dirty draught of creamy black.

And if the weather's balmy, sure you'll stay to celebrate,
You can always tell the wife a shower of bowsies made you
late.

Sláinte agus saol.
Sláinte agus saol,
Sláinte, sláinte agus saol.

PHILOMENA *now appears in the Palace Bar.* TRISTRAM
sees her immediately.

TRISTRAM (*spoken*).
Hello again, fancy meeting you.
Small world –

PHILOMENA.
Yes, isn't that true?

TRISTRAM.
Strange we should meet so frequently.

PHILOMENA.
Suppose it's destiny.

TRISTRAM.
A drink, perhaps?

PHILOMENA.
I don't know . . .
If you know what I suspect you know –
Even so, no, I should go.

She hands him a card.

My address – now I have to trot,
Maybe we'll talk some time,
Maybe not.

PHILOMENA *disappears.*

TRISTRAM.
Clearly she was rattled by my presence.
Even ready to do a deal, perhaps.
Anyway, time to check in at Betjeman's office.
Time I took a shot
At these poem-coded messages –
See what we've got.
An interesting day so far.
And that's before I'd even heard
'Me Jaunty Jarvey's Car'.

Scene Fourteen

Back in the British Office. BETJEMAN *is happily singing a tune he heard earlier on the radio.*

Song: **ME JAUNTY JARVEY'S CAR** – *stage-Irish, Percy-French feel.*

BETJEMAN.
    In me jaunty jarvey's car
    I chase the praties near and far;
    Drink shillelaghs at the bar,
    Shenanigans me Blarney-o!

    That's how leprechaun I've been!
    Some begorrahs I have seen,
    Mary is me own crubeen,
    In me jarvey's car I mean!

TRISTRAM (*spoken*).
    As I tried to read the messages
    Betjeman sang some utterly cretinous
    Doggerel that went on and on
    How long how long how long how long –

BETJEMAN.
    La-la-la-la, lah lah,
    La-la, praties, la-la-lah,
    La-la-la-la, lah lah,
    Top o' the evenin', Faraday!
    La-la-la-la, lah lah,
    La-la-la-la, lah lah lah.

TRISTRAM (*spoken*).
    Hard as I tried to con-cen-trate
    The relevant landscape filled with praties
    Shamrocks leprechauns diddly dye-dly –
    Why is he there just wittering idly?
    Block it all out just read the document,
    Read the leprechaun, and again shenanigan –

BETJEMAN.
    In me jaunty jarvey's car,
    La-la-la-la, lah lah lah,
    Drink shillelaghs at the bar,
    La-la-la-la, lah lah lah.

Two IRISH COLLEENS, *in full Irish-dancing regalia, appear from both sides of the stage, dancing in jig-time to the music.*

TRISTRAM (*sung*).
 Shocument, la, la, doprecaun, crubeen,
 Jigging in my head, diddle di eye, Philomena,
 Word associating in me old cawbogue,
 And shillelaghs at the bar? Shillelaghs at the bar!

The DANCERS *form a line either side of* TRISTRAM.

 I've been looking for a poem but a song comes along,
 And it could be the key; I don't know I could be wrong,
 Work it out work it out work it out!

TRISTRAM *begins dancing in time with the others.*

 Number all the letters that we find in the phrase:
 Drink shillelaghs at the bar, so we start with the A's.
 So the A in shillelagh's number one, there we are;
 Number two is in at, number three is in bar,

 On to the B that's in bar, that's four,
 Then the Ds, and the Es, moving on once more.
 Now these jumbled numbers are the anagram key.
 Apply them to your letters and reorder them sequentially.

The music stops suddenly as the DANCERS *dance offstage.*

 (*Spoken.*) By George the Sixth, I've got it!
 Yes! This message reads:
 'Pat getting out of hand. Probability bad.'
 Pat! Any idea who that could be?

BETJEMAN.
 The name scarcely narrows the field.

TRISTRAM.
 'Me Jaunty Jarvey's Car', where have I heard . . . ?

 Then suddenly, all was revealed.

 Transcripts! Transcripts of all the messages we've got!
 O'Dromedary's list of songs,
 I'll need to see the lot.

As BETJEMAN *hands* TRISTRAM *songsheets,*
TRISTRAM *starts breaking down the words. He's now on
home ground, assured, intent and slightly mad.*

BETJEMAN.
 Let me see, 'Oft In Darkling Groves Entwined' –

TRISTRAM.
 G-r-o, gor, ve, drak, krad, rove, love, glove, volg. Hmm,
 could be . . .

BETJEMAN.
Are you all right?

TRISTRAM.
Hm! Next song.

Intrigued by TRISTRAM's *behaviour,* BETJEMAN *hands him another page.*

Hm! Yes! Now if this, then, hm! But – Damn! More songs! The 'a' in here ah, ah, ah! Three, move that 'b' – yes! Faster!

Frantically, TRISTRAM *takes pages from* BETJEMAN.

And 'o', twenty-seven, over there, ng! Rrr! Uff! Ba-ba-ba – yes!

Pah! Het! Tuh! Pat, someone called Pat keeps – wait, I've skipped a 'u'. There! Yes, now we're – Oh, yes, oh, yes, come to Papa . . .

BETJEMAN.
Can I get you some water or any –

TRISTRAM.
Sh! Right, there's a lot of technical jargon of some kind. (*Reads.*) 'New pipes have somewhat eased pressure in the adjustment chamber . . . plentiful supply of feed water . . . constant vigilance still necessary or probability deeply unstable. Pat extremely temperamental and, I fear, dangerous, but our work, I am now convinced, is vital. Any suggestions more than welcome.'

Pat?

BETJEMAN.
No idea.

TRISTRAM.
(*Reads another message.*) 'Suggest damping down the backup valves, they're the lads could cost lives in the long run. Need hardly stress the importance of lubricant. Motor oil if you must, but there's nothing wrong with 3-in-1 at all at all. Without a doubt our work is vital, and Pat provides us with a small glimmer of hope in these dark times.'

Who are these people? And who is Pat?

(*Reads another message.*) 'Bad day today. Tank desperately unstable. Narrowly avoided the spiral we've long feared.

Hope we haven't pushed this whole business too far.'

(*Reads another message.*) 'The British may be onto us.
Someone called Faraday arrived today, more than likely a
spy. Must never find out about Pat.'

How ingenious!
Two people want to send each other coded messages
And for some reason they must never meet.
But for security they need to change their code keys every
    day.
So they agree on – yes, it looks like the third song played
Each evening on O'Dromedary's show.

Schrödinger!
He wanted to know what songs O'Dromedary had played!
That's because the announcer was moved to a morning show,
Which Schrödinger missed.
What's Schrödinger up to though?
We need to go and see him.

BETJEMAN.
    No, we need to wait till we know more.

The STAFF *of the British Office appear from beneath the bar.*

Song: **DIPLOMACY** – *music-hall, conspiratorial feel.*

BETJEMAN *and* STAFF (*sung*).
    Diplomacy, diplomacy,
    Mustn't go in in a rush.
    We'll put the knife in presently,
    Till then we'll smile incessantly
    And keep the whole thing tactfully
    And pleasantly hush hush!

BETJEMAN (*spoken*).
    Schrödinger's here at de Valera's invitation.
    If Schrödinger's up to something,
    With the Irish government's complicity,
    It could have consequences for Ireland's neutrality,
    A neutrality which Churchill might denounce,
    But which rather suits us none the less.
    Ireland's military resources are paltry,
    And if they were to side with us,
    We'd need to commit
    Some of our overstretched forces over here.
    So let's wait till we find out more.

Song: **MOLLY MAYHEM** – *nightmarish nursery rhyme.*

BETJEMAN.
Faraday, you ought to know,
Recently, the rumours go,
The IRA have someone new,
Energetic, cunning too.

TRISTRAM.
Any clue who he might be?

BETJEMAN.
No, except that he's a she.
Just a warning, to prepare you,
Should this floozie try to snare you.

She's popularly known
As Molly Mayhem, I believe,
Her real name's a mystery so far.
We don't know what she looks like,
We suspect that she's insane,
As Britain's enemies so often are.

Nightmare versions of AGENT GREEN *and* PHILOMENA
appear on table tops, tempting TRISTRAM, *siren-like. The
sing the line 'Molly Mayhem' repeatedly over the following:*

BETJEMAN *and* STAFF.
Molly Mayhem,
Whisper that name.
An informer's remains
Were found blocking a drain.
Molly Mayhem,
Does she exist?
Is it true she can kill
With a flick of her wrist?

BETJEMAN (*spoken*).
A stifled shriek, frantic scrambling down a country lane,
And soon a thud, and everybody knows
Molly Mayhem's just lopped off some dead wood.
Beguiling, ruthless and relentless;
Her eyes are everywhere,
Unblinking in the flickering dark,
Knows our every move,
And waits, and waits.

BETJEMAN *and* STAFF (*sung*).
> Molly Mayhem,
> A beauty they say,
> And a new figurehead
> In the IRA.
> Molly Mayhem,
> A mad harridan
> When she smells the blood
> Of an Englishman.

BETJEMAN *and the* STAFF *exit as the nightmare vision disappears.*

Scene Fifteen

TRISTRAM *is alone onstage.*

TRISTRAM.
> There's no time for hesitation,
> Now I know her bloody game,
> First the wireless dedication,
> Mentioned Philomena's name.
> Then the Red Bank Restaurant,
> She was there on some pretence.
> The Palace Bar, the wireless station –
> Now it all makes sense!
>
> Now the way ahead is clear.
> Fire in the belly here –
> Go to Philomena's place,
> Meet the viper face to face.
>
> So I make my way to her
> Digs on the North Circular.
> I see she can't conceal her fright,
> When I burst in there, late at night –
> Surprised myself, I have to say,
> Taking things in hand this way –
> Throwing off all self-restraint
> I overturn a plaster saint.

Scene Sixteen

PHILOMENA*'s flat.* PHILOMENA *appears, deshabillé.*

Song: INTERROGATION BOLERO.

The melody of this song allows space for PHILOMENA *to throw in protestations between the lines: 'Tristram', 'What do you mean?' etc. During the chorus,* PHILOMENA *also underscores with a Bolero-like 'bop-bop-a-bop-bo' line.*

TRISTRAM.
      Thought you'd get away with it,
      Thought I was an idiot,
      Thought you'd play your games with me,
      Thought I'd be too blind to see –

PHILOMENA.
      Can't just burst into my room –

TRISTRAM.
      Molly Mayhem, I presume?
      Tell me when did you begin
      Planning how to do me in?

CHORUS.
      Tell me, Philomena,
      Won't you tell me, Philomena?

TRISTRAM.
      The sky was overcast today.
      Tell me, will it stay that way?
      Or will it clear up suddenly?
      What would your prediction be?

PHILOMENA.
      Oh, my God, you've found me out!

TRISTRAM.
      'How Clear the Sky Above', no doubt?

PHILOMENA.
      You heard me asking for that song!

TRISTRAM.
      Well then, tell me, am I wrong?

CHORUS.
      Tell me, Philomena,
      Won't you tell me, Philomena?

      You use O'Dromedary's show
      To let the German bombers know

When the weather's suitable
For bombing us to bloody hell.

How do you predict it though?
How the blazes do you know
What the weather's going to be?
That's the thing that puzzles me.

CHORUS.
Tell me, Philomena,
Won't you tell me, Philomena?

PHILOMENA.
I don't predict the weather here;
The truth is even scarier.
How did you catch on to me?
You only got here recently.
Jesus, you're a British spy!

TRISTRAM.
Why I'm here is by the by.
Tell me what you have to say.

PHILOMENA.
You won't believe me anyway.

CHORUS.
Tell me, Philomena,
Won't you tell me, Philomena?

PHILOMENA.
You're a spy, can that be true?
And so full of passion, too.

TRISTRAM.
Watch it now, I won't be tricked –

PHILOMENA.
For a start, I don't predict:
The weather doesn't influence,
My choice of music in that sense,
Crazy as I'm bound to sound,
It's the other way around.

TRISTRAM (*spoken*).
What?

PHILOMENA (*spoken*).
The songs influence the weather.

A shift in the rhythm, then –

Song: **THE BEDTIME JIG.** *When* TRISTRAM *is speaking, the 'Oh!'s are* PHILOMENA*'s, and vice versa.*

TRISTRAM *and* PHILOMENA *climb onto the bar together and get frisky.*

TRISTRAM.
(Oh!) And suddenly, how shall I put it?
A rather astonishing turn of events.
Hard to believe but it just sort of happened,
And really it (Oh!) doesn't make any sense.
Let's say that I didn't go home as intended,
Not till the (Oh!) till the morning at least,
She overcame her religious convictions
And (Ah!) I'm afraid I was rather a beast.
But while I was with her my – God Almighty!
My thoughts were (Oh!) were racing about,
As I tried to make sense of my mission so far
And the (Oh!) the stuff I had yet to work out.

PHILOMENA.
I'm not looking forward to going to confession;
God bless us, I wouldn't know where to begin.
Infiltrated by British intelligence,
Oxymoronic as well as a sin.

TRISTRAM.
Have I walked into a honey trap here?
(Oh!) I ought to be watching my back.
Why is this chaste, religious girl
So incredibly good in the sack?

PHILOMENA.
This is so personal! What am I doing?
(Oh!) Sure I won't call a halt to it yet.
But how will I feel about this in the morning?
A sin to remember? A shame to forget?

TRISTRAM.
And I'm pounding away, and I'm pounding away
At this bloody delectable body of hers.

PHILOMENA.
(Oh!) Steady now, steady now, (Oh!)
Got to stay in the saddle to earn your spurs.

TRISTRAM.
Honey trap, honey trap, honey trap, (Oh!)

PHILOMENA.

In bed with a spy, in bed with a spy –

BOTH.

Oh, the guilt, the guilt, the guilt –

PHILOMENA.

In bed with a spy, how intriguing am I?

TRISTRAM.

I'll have to tell Green about breaking the code,
Quite an achievement to break it.
I pictured Green and how happy she'd be
Then I (Oh!) I pictured her naked.
Whoah, batten the (Oh!) the hatches,
I can't disappoint Philomena!
Let's face it, this (Oh!) this espionage
Is a tricky and deadly arena.
Schrödinger's messages, (Oh!) come on!
Try to work out what they (Oh!) what they meant,
(Oh!) And to whom they (Oh!) to whom they (Oh!
Oh! Oh!) To whom they were sent.
(Oh!) The messages –
(Oh!) The messages –
Think of the messages –
(Oh!) Think of England!

BOTH.

Oh, the guilt, the guilt, the guilt,
Oh! Oh! Oh! Oh!

TRISTRAM.

Oh, the messages! Oh, the messages!

PHILOMENA.

I feel so mysterious! Oh! Oh!

TRISTRAM.

I feel imperious! Oh! Oh!

BOTH.

Oh, Oh, Oh, Oh!
Ohhhhhhh!

Blackout.

ACT TWO

Scene One

It's morning. TRISTRAM *and* PHILOMENA *are perched on the bar.*

PHILOMENA.
Myles had been acting strangely for a while. He brought a wireless set in to work and was always bent over it, listening to O'Dromedary's programme and furiously taking notes. So then I started listening to it, too. And I noticed, I suppose, the same thing MI5 did. That the songs seemed to forecast the weather. This was the most appalling thing I'd ever heard!

TRISTRAM.
Giving help to the Nazis.

PHILOMENA.
Oh, that too, of course, but compromising Ireland's neutrality! Neutrality is an ethos poor Mr de Valera has worked so hard to uphold. But giving help to the Nazis, yes, that's definitely bad too, when you think about it.

TRISTRAM.
So why were you requesting songs that mentioned the weather?

PHILOMENA.
Well, obviously, to confuse whoever was listening! I'd pick a song on purpose that mentioned weather the exact opposite to the prevailing conditions. But gradually, I began to realise the most extraordinary thing. As soon as a song was played, the weather would change to match it.

TRISTRAM.
That's impossible.

PHILOMENA.
That's what I thought. I refused to believe it for ages, but every request confirmed it. So far the weather has matched the songs every time.

TRISTRAM.
But . . . how do you think O'Dromedary does it?

PHILOMENA.

It's not O'Dromedary. I don't think he's even aware of it. If he was, surely he'd want to choose what songs were played?

TRISTRAM.

Hm. So who – ?

PHILOMENA.

I don't know. But obviously Myles knows something about it. That's why I followed him to the Red Bank that night. And that's where I saw you . . .

TRISTRAM.

You didn't think I might have some involvement?

PHILOMENA.

Oh, Tristram, of course not!

TRISTRAM.

My darling.

PHILOMENA.

Whoever's behind this is fiendishly clever.

TRISTRAM.

Ah.

PHILOMENA.

Oh, no offence.

TRISTRAM.

None taken. Now, that night –

PHILOMENA.

I mean, I know you're very fast at the crosswords.

TRISTRAM.

Yes, all right. That night in the Red Bank, before you arrived, O'Dromedary played a request for a Philomena.

PHILOMENA.

Really?

TRISTRAM.

Said she'd 'lie beside our foreign friend'.

PHILOMENA.

Oh. Wonder what that's about?

TRISTRAM.

So then you appeared, and . . .

PHILOMENA.
That's what happened, isn't it?

TRISTRAM.
What?

PHILOMENA.
Last night. 'Lie beside our foreign friend.'

TRISTRAM.
Well, yes . . .

PHILOMENA.
So, when I turned up, you thought I was some mysterious conspirator?

TRISTRAM.
And then I kept running into you.

PHILOMENA.
Because we were obviously on the same trail. And I followed you into the Palace Bar yesterday. I thought maybe you were about to break the story in your newspaper, and I wanted to persuade you not to, for neutrality's sake. I chickened out, though.

TRISTRAM.
Maybe . . . maybe we could meet in the Palace again tonight? And you could stay for a drink this time?

PHILOMENA.
I . . . I don't know. Would you like to?

TRISTRAM.
More than anything else.

They kiss.

PHILOMENA.
Right, so . . .

TRISTRAM.
I should go.

PHILOMENA.
No, stay a while, I mean, if you want to . . . here, I'll stick the wireless on.

O'DROMEDARY*'s voice booms out.*

O'DROMEDARY (*recorded*).
And think of Philomena now,
For her hour is coming soon.

She'll come through when the chips are down
At the rising of the moon.

PHILOMENA.
My God!

O'DROMEDARY.
And then we'll see some changes,
My friends, believe you me,
Some major alterations in all probability.

TRISTRAM.
My God!

A distant boom of thunder.

Probability . . . probability. That word . . . it occurred in the
messages so many times! What am I doing here? Cold coils
up my spine. How could I have been so blind? Are we all in
mortal danger? What am I doing here, wasting time? Must
find Agent Green. Pray God this isn't so.

PHILOMENA.
Tristram, are you all right?

TRISTRAM.
I really have to go.

PHILOMENA.
Oh. Say, five o'clock, so?

TRISTRAM.
What?

PHILOMENA.
The Palace Bar?

TRISTRAM.
Oh, yes, yes.

PHILOMENA.
Tristram!

TRISTRAM.
Yes, five o'clock.

PHILOMENA.
I've just thought of something! The Philomena he
mentioned in that request –

TRISTRAM.
Yes?

PHILOMENA.

A few days ago I had to process a compensation claim. A trawler, the Philomena, had been stolen. Of course everyone had a pretty good idea it was the IRA took it.

TRISTRAM.

A trawler?

PHILOMENA.

'Lie beside our foreign friend'? A rendezvous of some kind? Maybe with the Germans?

TRISTRAM (*distracted*).

Yes, a trawler . . . Germans . . . hm, I suppose that's possible. Now, really, I must go.

PHILOMENA.

Tristram!

TRISTRAM.

Yes, what is it?

PHILOMENA.

Meet me in the Palace Bar
At five o'clock, then we can talk.

TRISTRAM.

Well, yes, although in my position,
Mustn't jeopardise my mission,
Got to keep this quite discreet,
But yes, we'll meet, be sure of that.
But now I've got to go and find . . .
Well, let's call him Pat.

He leaves.

Song: **LIKE LOVERS DO THESE DAYS** – *light, airy melody, slightly Latin feel.*

PHILOMENA.

Meet me in the Palace Bar
At five o'clock, then we can talk,
Only tell me what you want to,
Nowadays that's how things are.
We'll drink, and skirt around our secrets
In the Palace Bar.

We can get to know each other,
Whispering in the smoky haze,
At least that much is in our power,

Living for the next half-hour –
Like lovers do these days.

I know you're only new in town,
And I'm an ingénue in town,
Still I swear I'll be with you
No matter what I have to do,
When the chips are down,
When the chips are down.

So meet me in the Palace Bar,
We'll whisper and we'll look both ways,
Alert to every tiny change,
Alert to anything that's strange –
Like lovers are these days,
Like lovers are these days.

PHILOMENA *wanders off into darkness.*

Scene Two

TRISTRAM *reappears. He is alone.*

TRISTRAM.
Who sent the messages?
Schrödinger, I'm sure of that.
Why else would he want to know
What songs O'Dromedary had played?
But who he's been corresponding with,
Regarding Pat?
I've no idea, I'm afraid.

Probability.
His work relates to probability.
Sub-atomic particles – or waves –
And their trajectory.
Sub-atomic.

Never mind who Pat might be,
Something had occurred to me,
And wouldn't go away.
An atomic scientist
In a neutral country – Ireland, say –
Mightn't he be free to work
Unhindered, secretly,
Conveniently distant

From proper scrutiny?
And what might he be working on
So far from prying eyes?
Maybe an atomic device!

Strange, post-apocalyptic CREATURES *with flashing atoms growing from their heads pop up from beneath the bar. They sing.*

Song: **AN IRISH ATOM BOMB** – *relentless march-of-science feel.*

ALL.

Do the Irish have an atom bomb?
The genocidal grail?
A licence for unruliness
On an exponential scale?
Think about the consequences
If that should be right –

TRISTRAM.

And I wonder was I just
A little indiscreet last night?

ALL.

Do the Irish have an atom bomb?
What consequences loom?
I'll have to try and find a way
Of staving off our doom.

TRISTRAM.

Not a word to Philomena,
I can't quite trust her yet,
And I'm wondering if last night
Is something I might soon regret.

Over the following the heads appear and disappear beneath the bar in slow, wave-like patterns.

(*Spoken.*) O'Dromedary: does he wield
Some monstrous influence?
It seems absurd despite
The circumstantial evidence.
Radio waves, that was what
He more than hinted at,
But Christ, an Irish atom bomb,
And who the hell is Pat?

Betjeman would hesitate
And do things by the book.
Prevaricate and vacillate
And let them off the hook.
I'll have to let him know, of course,
But now is not the time.
Show the man an atom bomb,
He'll want to find a rhyme.

No, I've got to go to Green
And tell her my suspicions.
She'll know how to handle this
Most tricky of positions.
She and I might have a chance
Of putting this thing right.
No time now to think about
The fun I had last night.

The heads disappear. TRISTRAM *is joined by* GREEN.

GREEN.
Do the Irish have an atom bomb?
Hold me, I feel queasy.

TRISTRAM.
I know, it's just a nightmare –

GREEN.
No, Tristram, take it easy!
This is more than we could hope for,
No ifs or buts:
If Ireland have an atom bomb,
We've got them by the nuts.

Let me question Schrödinger,
I'll make him sing I swear.

She produces a pistol.

TRISTRAM.
Jesus!

GREEN.
There's a war on, Tristram,
Weren't you aware?

She beckons him to follow her. As they move off, the lights change and a few bars of 'Inner Specialness'.
PHILOMENA *enters the Palace Bar and sits at one of the tables.*

The lights come back up on TRISTRAM *and* GREEN, *as they near the Institute of Advanced Studies, where Schrödinger works.*

GREEN.
The trawler Philomena –
Yes, that's plausible, all right.
Explains that radio request
We heard the other night.

TRISTRAM *and* GREEN *do a little circuit, making their way to the bar.*

They're running guns, I reckon,
And we'll deal with that in time.
But Christ, an Irish atom bomb!
Now isn't that sublime?

TRISTRAM.
This is the Institute here.

GREEN.
An open window at the rear.
The hour of glory's near, my dear.

TRISTRAM.
Good luck, be careful!

GREEN.
Never fear!

They climb over the bar to enter.

Scene Three

The spotlights blaze on to reveal SCHRÖDINGER *playing a theremin. He is stroking it, almost seducing it.*

SCHRÖDINGER.
Who . . . ?

GREEN.
Herr Schrödinger. We meet at last.

SCHRÖDINGER.
Good evening, Fräulein . . . ?

GREEN.
Where's the bomb?

SCHRÖDINGER.
> I've no idea what you mean –
> Where on earth did you come from?

GREEN.
> The atom bomb! We know it's here!
> We know what you've been at.

TRISTRAM.
> The project you've been working on,
> And somebody called Pat.

SCHRÖDINGER.
> Pat? How do you know that name?

TRISTRAM.
> I figured out your code.

GREEN.
> Come on! The bomb! Just lead the way,
> And show us where it's stowed.

TRISTRAM.
> Take it easy!

GREEN.
> Where's the bomb?

SCHRÖDINGER.
> There is no bomb, I swear.
> And PAT is not somebody,
> PAT is . . . something, over there.
>
> It seems I have no choice
> But to reveal our little scheme –
> By the way, your body
> Is a filthy schoolboy's dream.

GREEN.
> Shut up! So if it's not a bomb,
> What is it? What is that?

SCHRÖDINGER.
> Very well, let me tell you,
> Let me show you . . . PAT.

A wheel appears behind the bar and when SCHRÖDINGER
turns it, the pillars of the GPO rotate backwards becoming
vast cannons pointing towards the audience and revealing a
huge fantastical machine, with numerous flashing lights and
pulsating tanks behind the portico. As SCHRÖDINGER
sings, it hums and belches with electronic activity.

Presumably this is what you came to see?
By the way, it's an acronym – PAT.

TRISTRAM *and* GREEN.
Good God!
What is it?
What does it do?

SCHRÖDINGER.
An ingenious device, wait, I'll tell you.

Song: **AN INGENIOUS DEVICE** – *spoken in rhythm by all.*

SCHRÖDINGER.
I said to de Valera, very early in the war,
You are neutral, by the book, and to the letter,
But diplomacy alone is not sufficient any more
Some sub-atomic physics might be better.

TRISTRAM.
What did you mean?

GREEN.
Some kind of weapon?

SCHRÖDINGER.
We never thought of weapons, to be frank.
The miracle you see
Is not some silly piece of weaponry,
But a Probability Adjustment Tank.

TRISTRAM *and* GREEN.
Good God!

SCHRÖDINGER.
It bends the laws of probability,
Bends them that way, and this way, and that –

TRISTRAM *and* GREEN.
Oh, no!

SCHRÖDINGER.
So you see why I say in all humility,
Ireland is neutral today thanks to PAT.

TRISTRAM.
How fiendish!

GREEN.
How galling!

SCHRÖDINGER.
Well, possibly, from your point of view, I suppose.

GREEN.
Under our noses! The whole thing's appalling!

TRISTRAM.
The coded messages, who was sending those?

SCHRÖDINGER.
An amateur enthusiast advises me, it's true,
And you can't imagine what a help he's been.
What genius dilettante am I so beholden to?
Why, obviously Myles na gCopaleen.

TRISTRAM *and* GREEN.
Good God!

SCHRÖDINGER.
The waves of altered probability
Shoot through the pipes and away they go –

TRISTRAM *and* GREEN.
Oh, no!

SCHRÖDINGER.
To the GPO, from there to be
Broadcast over the radio.

TRISTRAM.
O'Dromedary! The waves! Oh, please,
No, pray God, this can't be so!
These altered probabilities
Are nightly threaded through his show!
Making his every turn of phrase
A sinister reality.

SCHRÖDINGER.
Ah! Maybe that's the price one pays,
It's worth it for neutrality.

The music stops.

TRISTRAM.
A Probability Adjustment Tank, of course!
And that's why Myles was always in the Red Bank –
It's the only pub in town where you know
You'll hear O'Dromedary's show on the radio!

GREEN *reveals a long rope.*

GREEN.

Never mind that now, something bigger's at stake.
I think it's pretty clear what action we ought to take:
Whenever there's a crisis, everyone has a role,
And we Brits have a duty to take control.

TRISTRAM *and* GREEN *perform a rope-dance around the bar, tying* SCHRÖDINGER *up as they go.*

Song: **IMPERIAL TANGO.**

GREEN.

In situations such as these,
In any crisis small or large,
It's vital everyone agrees –

TRISTRAM *and* GREEN.

The British ought to be in charge.

TRISTRAM.

When there's division anywhere,
The thing you have to understand
Is that it's simply right and fair –

TRISTRAM *and* GREEN.

To let the British take command.

TRISTRAM.

We really ought to utilise
This rather wonderful device,
It seems our sneaky Irish hosts
Were using it to shift the posts.

GREEN.

A thing we British can't condone,
At least until we've got one of our own.

TRISTRAM *and* GREEN.

Grant us patience when these nations'
Notions so exceed their stations,
And their crafty machinations
Sour all hope of good relations.
Shame on you for what you've done,
You've only gone and lowered the bloody tone.

TRISTRAM.

Don't run about like headless chickens.

SCHRÖDINGER.

Bauk, bauk, bauk, bauk, bauk, bauk, bauk, bauk.

GREEN.
You're sitting ducks, accept your fate.

SCHRÖDINGER.
Quack, quack, quack, quack, quack, quack, quack, quack.

TRISTRAM *and* GREEN.
Oh, how the British heartbeat quickens.

SCHRÖDINGER.
La, la, la, la, la, la, la, la.

TRISTRAM *and* GREEN.
When we have foreigners to berate.

SCHRÖDINGER.
Cha, cha, cha, cha, cha, cha, cha, cha.

*Over an instrumental break, they hoist SCHRÖDINGER
aloft above the bar and begin to adjust the various dials,
levers and pedals of the tank. There is a loud noise.*

Mein Gott!

Now probability's upended.
Please won't you let me get my tools.
I must attend the tank and mend it,
Before it stalls between two fools.

GREEN.
No time to put things to the test now –

TRISTRAM.
No time to diagnose the sickness –

GREEN.
The quick solution is the best now –

TRISTRAM *and* GREEN.
It always is, in terms of quickness.

Don't fret: the Brits are in control now;
We're rather good in a disaster.
So just admit you're in a hole now,
And we can help you dig much faster.

*TRISTRAM and GREEN get quite playful while adjusting
the tank. By the end of the song, she has backed him into a
chair. Suddenly MULDOON appears from behind the bar,
and handcuffs TRISTRAM to the chair.*

TRISTRAM.
What are you doing?

GREEN.
>You poor fool!
>Our plot has reached fruition.
>A German U-boat's on its way
>With guns and ammunition.

MULDOON.
>She'll meet the Philomena
>In Lough Foyle tonight,
>And then we'll strike the *Sassenach*
>With all our might.

GREEN.
>Our boys await the signal;
>They'll be sailing very soon,
>But not till O'Dromedary plays
>'The Rising of the Moon'.

TRISTRAM.
>It's you! The mystery woman
>Who's been causing such a stir.
>The mastermind we heard about –
>You're her!

>*Song:* **BETRAYAL** – *histrionic cabaret feel.*

GREEN (*spoken*).
>Espionage is dirty work,
>And many hidden perils lurk.
>But looming there behind them all
>You'll find the poisoned bloom we call –
>
>(*Sung.*) Betrayal . . .
>Isn't it divine?
>To step across the line
>Unforgivably –
>
>Betrayal . . .
>It's not so good for you,
>But what are we to do?
>It's fabulous for me!

SCHRÖDINGER (*spoken*).
>The British tolerate
>The neutral Free State,
>But try to mount a coup
>And they'll be all over you!

MULDOON.
Let them come, we're ready,
And to hell with de Valera,
With a little German help we'll
Build a better Éire.

GREEN.
Now you see how dumb you've been,
It's time to take it on the chin.
You see how easily you fall
Before the poisoned bloom they call –

(*Sung.*) Betrayal . . .
Isn't it divine?
To step across that line
Unforgiveably –

Betrayal . . .
It's not so good for you,
But what are we to do?
It's fabulous for me!

TRISTRAM *begins to grapple with the handcuffs, trying to free himself.*

(*To* MULDOON.) Darling, break it to him
Why he oughtn't interfere?

MULDOON (*approaching* TRISTRAM).
Nothing will be broken
Gently here.

MULDOON *retreats behind the bar and returns wearing a tool belt complete with various instruments of torture.* GREEN *opens a varnished box containing further instruments and displays them proudly to the audience like prizes on a game show.*

Song: **WE HAVE TO DO THESE THINGS RIGHT** – *haunting bar-ballad feel.*

MULDOON.
So you cottoned on to our game.
Smart boy wanted, fair do's.
A worthy foe,
But even so,
I wouldn't be in your shoes.

Settle down now, sit tight.
It's going to be a long, long night.

I'll need to choose
Which tools to use.
We have to do these things right.

MULDOON *and* GREEN.
Softly, softly,
Destiny calls us tonight.
Gently, gently,
We two must do this right.

Lights up on PHILOMENA *in the Palace Bar. She sings, to the same (or similar) tune.*

PHILOMENA.
It's late now, I really should go.
Tristram, why didn't you show?
Why'd you leave me
High and dry?
I don't suppose I'll ever know.

Lights up on GREEN *in the Institute.*

GREEN.
You were too easy by far.
I'd click my fingers and there you'd be –
A pawn, a dupe,
But now you see,
You've jumped through your last hoop for me.

PHILOMENA *and* GREEN.
Tristram, Tristram,
Time's run out, finally.
No hard feelings –
Soon you'll be a memory.

MULDOON.
The trawler Philomena sails out,
She'll meet with a U-boat, my friend,
And bring back guns
For Ireland's sons –
But that won't concern you by then.

Hacksaw, razors –
Maybe I'll heat up a pan –
Knives or scissors,
A night of pain is your only man.

MULDOON *begins to torture* TRISTRAM.

Song: **GOD'S BICYCLE SLIPPED A GEAR** – *unhinged relentless sing-song.*

TRISTRAM (*spoken*).
Muldoon worked at a careful pace –
The word painstaking seems to fit,
Measuring each dig and jab
And probing bit by bloody bit.

We see MULDOON *make some sudden, ominously invasive movement.*

Then something happened: a tiny jolt,
And everything was altered here,
Subtly, fundamentally,
As though God's bike had slipped a gear.

CHORUS.
God's bicycle slipped a gear,
Slipped a gear, slipped a gear.
God's bicycle slipped a gear,
Slipped a gear, slipped.

TRISTRAM (*spoken*).
And now it's all what might have been,
I feel myself succumb,
Little by little, but faster and faster,
A rolling stone gathers momentum.

Chorus.

TRISTRAM (*spoken*).
God's bicycle slipped a gear,
Pain will do funny things, it's true,
Except in this particular case,
I knew the others felt it, too.

MULDOON.
Did it just get cold in here?

GREEN.
No, I'd say it got cold, if anything.

The tank rumbles ominously.

MULDOON.
I thought you knew how to work the tank,
But look, it's smouldering.

SCHRÖDINGER.
Too much improbability

Is mounting up too fast.
O'Dromedary's studio is getting the full blast.

Chorus.

MULDOON.
Don't worry, pet, we'll be all right,
Whatever this machine might do.
No need to fret, just hold on tight –
Me and you, we'll see this through

GREEN.
So tender underneath the rough!
Can anything stand in your way?
What bombshell would have power enough –
Apart from what I'm about to say –

MULDOON.
Eh?

GREEN *shoots* MULDOON.

No!

Song: **BETRAYAL** (*reprise*).

GREEN (*spoken*).
Sorry darling, so unjust,
But silly you to put your trust
In someone who is so in thrall
To the poisoned bloom they call –

(*Sung.*) Betrayal!
Isn't it such fun
To dash another one
Unexpectedly –
Betrayal!
Oh, the heady thrill!
Unbelievable,
It comes so easily.

(*Spoken.*) Very soon I'm going to be a heroine, you'll see:
My superiors will hear you're getting help from Germany,
And when that trawler puts ashore, you won't be neutral
    any more,
And the Brits will be in charge here, just like we were before.

MULDOON (*dying*).
What about us? And all the plans we had?
To strike a blow against your class, your country and your
    dad?

You're not going to tell me that that was all a lie.

GREEN.

Maybe not quite all, but please, shut up and die.

Tristram, should I free you? You see my position:
I'm very fond of you, but you know you lack ambition.
And I don't need you now my plot has reached fruition,
So bringing war to Ireland ought to stay a solo mission.

GREEN *begins to explore the various controls.*

What happens when I turn this dial? There now, we shall see.
I'll work this out, I mean, how complicated can it be?

SCHRÖDINGER.

I beg you!

GREEN.

No, just hang on there, and Tristram, you sit tight.
Just a few adjustments here; it should be quite a night.

Scene Four

MYLES *alone outside the Palace Bar, by the lamp post.*

MYLES.

The air isn't right tonight:
Some anomalous wavular activity
Engendering strange logomorphic manifestations,
Leaving the plain people banjaxed and bewildered.
Wouldn't be anything to do with the tank, I suppose?
Maybe I should pay Schrödinger a visit.

BETJEMAN *now arrives and greets* MYLES. *They perform
a gladiatorial routine, posturing on table tops.*

BETJEMAN.

Myles!

MYLES.

Ah, John, how's the spying racket?

BETJEMAN.

An ugly rumour. Spread by those who envy me my talent.

MYLES.

Isn't that shocking? That there are people out there who'd
regard you as talented?

Song: **YOU'LL WRITE SOMETHING BLOODY GOOD ONE DAY** – *music-hall duet.*

BETJEMAN.
Tell me, how's your funny column?
So amusing, never solemn,
Quite a rapier wit you've got,
Parochial, yes, but gosh, why not?
Keep at it, you keep beavering away.
I'm going to stick my neck out here and say,
That you'll write something bloody good one day.

MYLES.
Thank you, I'd be very flattered,
If I thought your judgement mattered.
Still and all, congratulations,
Bear in mind, not just your patience
But your awesome limitations,
I'd be churlish if I didn't say
That you'll write something bloody good one day.

BETJEMAN.
Satire wielded with precision,
Erudite and wicked vision.
Shame it's always undercut
With feeble puns and schoolboy smut.
But for your sake, I hope and pray
That you won't fritter all your gifts away –
And you'll write something bloody good one day.

MYLES.
Oh, how winsome; oh, how wistful;
Oh, the clichés by the fistful;
Oh, the simpering vignettes
Of life in leafy Middlesex!
Still, I think it's fair to say
The law of averages will have its way –
And you'll write something readable one day.

(*Spoken.*) Going to the Palace?

BETJEMAN (*spoken*).
Why not?

BETJEMAN *and* MYLES *enter the bar and see* PHILOMENA *sitting on her own.*

A comely maiden, on her own!
May I treat you to a sherry?

PHILOMENA.
Thanks, I'm happy here alone.

BETJEMAN.
Happy? Are you really?

PHILOMENA.
Very.

BETJEMAN.
Was some farmboy cruel and callous?
Or a boorish clerk perhaps?
Now you're stranded in the Palace,
With a bunch of drunken chaps?

MYLES.
Was it Faraday? The lout.

BETJEMAN.
Faraday? Ah, you're his gel!

PHILOMENA.
Never mind, I'm going out.
And Faraday can go to hell.

Song: **THE INNER SPECIALNESS OF ME** (*reprise*).

PHILOMENA.
The Palace Bar was empty, when I walked in;
My footsteps echoed out across the floor,
Sitting there, my spirits soared and fell again,
As each new face appeared around the door.
I've got a life that's rich with who knows what potential.
Why should I be loitering out here?
If I pay attention to the things that really count,
I may go up a grade within the year . . .

Then I think about last night, and oh, the way we kissed,
Sadly, it seems I have to cross him off my list,
I had hopes for better, but he clearly missed
The inner specialness of me.

As she turns to go, PHILOMENA *spots a* MAN *taking feathers from a newspaper wrapping, and trying to eat them.*

PHILOMENA (*spoken*).
What? Oh, no! But how –
I have to find him now.

O'DROMEDARY's voice can be heard again, but now we also see his face emanating, Wizard-of-Oz-like, from the tank.

O'DROMEDARY (*recorded*).
The kettle's on, so settle down,
And let the music soothe you now.
We've lots of songs to play for you,
And dedications too –

The music and lights suggest simultaneous power surges in the Institute and the studio. Around the walls of the space, cables begin to glow, and wires crackle. The waves of light increase their oscillations.

The waves! The waves!
The waves are in full flow!
I feel them coursing through me now,
I feel them come and go.
Surely all can feel it now,
The stirring in the atmosphere,
The waves are taking over now,
Or so it would appear.
I feel the waves are full of rage,
Some dark immense vexation,
But few can see the gravity
Of the situation.

Lights up on the bar. PHILOMENA *re-enters.*

MYLES.
Philomena –

PHILOMENA.
We've got to find Tristram!

We were supposed to meet. But first he had to see someone called Pat.

MYLES.
He's gone to see PAT? I see. I knew he was a spy.

PHILOMENA.
Is he in some kind of danger?

MYLES.
If he has a run-in with PAT, we all are.

BETJEMAN.
Are you going to tell us what's going on?

MYLES.

You'd better come with me. To the Institute for Advanced Studies. This could be serious. I'll explain on the way.

BETJEMAN.

The Institute isn't far. If we levitate we can get there by air in no time.

PHILOMENA.

What?

BETJEMAN.

Why are you looking at me like that? Is there some law against unaided human flight?

PHILOMENA.

Is this some kind of joke?

MYLES.

Obviously he doesn't understand the gravity of the situation . . . It's happening again. Acting out these phrases. My God! Could it be? PAT . . . the waves . . . O'Dromedary? Quickly! The Institute!

Lights up on the Institute. GREEN is adjusting one of the dials.

Spoken sequence: **WAHRSCHEINLICHKEITSSPIRALE.**

TRISTRAM.

Then, a curious thing happened. As I was trying to figure out a way to prevent the trawler Philomena from picking up a small consignment of arms from a German U-boat, there was a strange noise.

PAT makes an ominous noise.

GREEN.

What's that?

SCHRÖDINGER.

Oh, dear. It's a probability spiral.

GREEN.

A what?

SCHRÖDINGER.

Whatever you do, don't touch that lever. It would render the tank itself improbable.

O'DROMEDARY'*s face appears in the tank.*

O'DROMEDARY.
  A certain lady wants to hear
  A very special tune.

GREEN.
  This is it! He's going to play
  'The Rising of the Moon!'

SCHRÖDINGER.
  Never mind that! What's the reading on that dial?

GREEN.
  This one? Five.

SCHRÖDINGER.
  That's bad. Turn it to six.

GREEN.
  Done.

SCHRÖDINGER.
  No, I mean four!

  BANG.

GREEN.
  Noooo!

TRISTRAM.
  Then, a curious thing happened. As I was trying to figure
  out a way to prevent the trawler Philomena from picking up
  enough arms from a German U-boat to equip the entire IRA
  Northern command, there was a strange noise.

  Ominous noise.

GREEN.
  What's that?

SCHRÖDINGER.
  Oh, dear. It's a probability spiral.

GREEN.
  A what?

SCHRÖDINGER.
  Whatever you do, don't touch that lever. It would render the
  tank itself improbable.

  O'DROMEDARY's *face appears in the tank.*

O'DROMEDARY.
  A certain lady wants to hear
  A very special tune.

GREEN.
> This is it! He's going to play
> 'The Rising of the Moon'!

SCHRÖDINGER.
> Never mind that! What's the reading on that dial?

GREEN.
> This one? Six.

SCHRÖDINGER.
> What? That's impossible! This could change probabilities
> retrospectively and rupture the whole course of history. Tell
> you what, try turning it to seven.

GREEN.
> Done.

SCHRÖDINGER.
> No, I mean five!

BANG.

GREEN.
> Noooo!

TRISTRAM.
> Then, a curious thing happened. As I was reflecting on how
> much things had changed around here, there was a strange
> noise.

Ominous noise.

GREEN.
> Was war denn das?

SCHRÖDINGER.
> Ach, du meine Güte! Eine Wahrscheinlichkeitsspirale!

GREEN.
> Eine . . . wie bitte?

SCHRÖDINGER.
> Was immer Du machst, fass bloß nicht den Hebel da an.
> Damit würde der Tank selbst unwahrscheinlich werden.

O'DROMEDARY'*s face appears in the tank.*

O'DROMEDARY.
> Eine bestimmte Dame möchte gern
> Eine ganz besondere Melodie hören.

GREEN.
> Es ist soweit! Er spielt jetzt 'The Rising of the Moon'!

SCHRÖDINGER.

Lass das jetzt! Was steht auf dem Anzeiger??

GREEN.

Dem hier? Sieben.

SCHRÖDINGER.

Sieben? Naja. Sheep as a lamb. Stell ihn auf zehn.

MYLES, PHILOMENA *and* BETJEMAN *enter, surprising* GREEN. *There is a tussle.* GREEN *loses her gun, and makes an escape bid, into a chamber of the tank. Exhausted,* BETJEMAN *leans on the forbidden lever.*

No! The lever!

There is a loud bang. Pandemonium. O'DROMEDARY *appears in the tank.*

O'DROMEDARY.

A certain lady wants to hear
A very special . . . wait . . .
That's strange. I feel . . . intoxicated
Just from breathing (hic) breathing in.
They should bottle this . . . what do you call it?
Now, what was I supposed to . . .
Ah, who the hell cares?
I'll just take another deep breath and . . .

There's a sound of snoring.

BETJEMAN.

What's happened to him?

SCHRÖDINGER.

Clearly the density of the waves in the studio has caused a bizarre chemical reaction, rendering the oxygen in the air intoxicating.

MYLES.

Ah. The broadcaster's worst nightmare. He's drunk on air.

Lights up on PAT. More noise.

Quick! She's going to blow! You regulate the electron sorters, I'll grab hold of the likelihood wheel. Implausibility overload!

Huge noise, lights.

SCHRÖDINGER.

Vast waves of improbability . . . surging outwards, saturating every brick in Dublin.

MYLES.
Charging every atom with pure, unrefined unlikelihood.

SCHRÖDINGER.
This could render the whole city dangerously improbable
for decades to come.

MYLES.
Oh. Is that all?

*One last bang. Blackout. A long scream which continues as
the lights come back up.*

TRISTRAM.
Where's Green?

We see GREEN's *face in the tank. She is swirling deep into
the void.*

SCHRÖDINGER.
Hard to say. Sucked into a different set of probabilities.
Perhaps she was just too unlikely. Or not unlikely enough.

PHILOMENA *has untied* TRISTRAM.

TRISTRAM.
Thanks.

PHILOMENA.
Are you okay?

TRISTRAM.
Not too bad. So what made you decide to look for me?

PHILOMENA.
I almost didn't. I was on the point of going home, when
I saw a man eating feathers from a sheet of newspaper.

TRISTRAM.
So you deduced probabilities were running riot?

PHILOMENA.
Yes. And I'd promised I'd be with you when the chips were
down.

TRISTRAM.
And do you still feel that way?

PHILOMENA.
I don't know, Tristram. I've had a horrible thought. I can't
help wondering if you and I, and everything we did, might
have been done under the influence of O'Dromedary, or
PAT?

TRISTRAM.
No! No, it was more than that.

PHILOMENA.
How can we ever be sure?

MYLES.
Well, it looks like our game's up.

SCHRÖDINGER.
Yes, and if this gets out, I'll have to leave Ireland.

MYLES.
I'll have to leave the civil service.

BETJEMAN.
If this gets out, Ireland won't stay neutral.

PHILOMENA.
Oh, no!

BETJEMAN.
Er, Faraday?

TRISTRAM.
What?

SCHRÖDINGER.
We'd like to know where we stand.

TRISTRAM.
Of course. (*He looks to* PHILOMENA.) As would I.

PHILOMENA.
Ohhh. Well . . . Sunder love unfinished.

TRISTRAM.
What?

PHILOMENA.
It's a clue for you. Ten letters.

Scene Five

TRISTRAM *is isolated in a searchlight.*

TRISTRAM.
Sunder love unfinished.
I soon worked it out,
Then realised I shouldn't even
Have needed a clue.

When I got back to London,
I rested up a day or two.
My report, meanwhile,
Was sending quiet shockwaves through HQ.
Of course I'd mentioned PAT.
I could scarcely have avoided that.
And Éire's neutrality, I knew,
Would soon be a memory,
An improbability too far.

Debriefing time. The Colonel motioned me
Along a corridor,
Quite the celebrity now.
Heads turning, gauging my present status
And expected trajectory,
Recalibrating my usefulness,
And nodding shrewdly, yes.
Nobody's mentioned knighthood yet,
It's in the air, none the less.

The soft-spoken COLONEL *steps into the light. Two* AIDES
appear behind the bar.

Song: **WHAT DOES IT ALL MEAN?** – *music-hall feel,*
spoken in time with the music.

COLONEL.
    Bit crocked-up? Hard luck, old sport,
    But, scorching stuff in this report.
    And now you're on your feet perhaps
    You'd help me fill in certain gaps.

AIDE 1.
    Poor Green – ah, we had hopes for her,
    Rose through the ranks in a dizzying blur.
    A shame, but how were we to know
    That Ireland would corrupt her so?

AIDE 2.
    O'Dromedary – what a prat.
    Quit his post, thank God for that.
    So, yes, I've got the gist of it,
    Until we hit the science bit.

COLONEL.
    What does it mean?
    Did some pages blow away?
    I feel I've almost got it

Then my thoughts begin to stray.
This dread machine –
Please fill me in on that.
The story rather peters out
Just when we get to PAT.

TRISTRAM.

The tank? Yes, what I wrote is true,
I've witnessed what that thing can do –

COLONEL.

Fire away, then, I'm all ears –
Does this confirm our darkest fears?

TRISTRAM.

Gosh, well, Colonel, where to start?
No mistake, their plan was smart,
But then again we must take heart:
The thing was flawed and fell apart.

COLONEL.

It says so here – cause for cheer,
Although I fear I'm still unclear
What the gadget did, you see –
To alter probability?
What does it mean?
Please help me out, I'm stuck.
Is it decent British physics
Or the slippery foreign muck?
This dread machine –
Out with it now, old bean –
It alters probability,
But how? What does it mean?

TRISTRAM.

The principles are quite arcane
But let me try to make it plain:
Schrödinger, na gCopaleen,
Between them built this dread machine,
And what it did, well, here's the thing –

COLONEL.

Out with it, yes, we're listening!

TRISTRAM.

It had the capability
For making a whiskey instantly.

COLONEL.
> What do you mean?
> Can you say that once again?
> I swear I thought I heard
> A sheer absurdity just then.
> This dread machine –
> Surely you can't mean
> That all this fuss has been
> About a tank that makes poteen?

TRISTRAM.
> Exactly, sir – yes, I suppose
> Its name was slightly grandiose;
> It altered probability
> Quite locally, admittedly.

Scene Six

The lights change and TRISTRAM *is again isolated in the spot.*

TRISTRAM.
> I was quietly discharged, pensioned off.
> A tactfully unspecified infirmity.
> I'm not sure why I told the lie.
> Perhaps I was afraid someone would try
> To build the thing again.
> Perhaps this was just another large improbability,
> Part of the tank's lasting legacy.
> Or perhaps I'd had enough of spying,
> And didn't want to see Green's dream
> Of a reoccupied Ireland
> Coming true because of me.
> One thing I was certain of,
> I'd go back to Ireland as soon as I could.
> The answer to Philomena's clue held out
> Just enough encouragement for that.
> And maybe this was also
> A reason I'd lied about PAT.
> Maybe I'd come to realise
> It's sometimes best for things to be . . .
> To be . . .

Scene Seven

Lights up again on the Institute. This scene is a continuation of Scene Four.

TRISTRAM.
Ah. Got it. Unresolved.

BETJEMAN.
What?

MYLES.
The answer to her clue.

PHILOMENA.
Yes.

TRISTRAM.
I see.

PHILOMENA.
Maybe that's what it always has to be.

TRISTRAM.
Unresolved. I can live with that.

BETJEMAN.
That's what living is.

MYLES.
Unresolved isn't the worst. At least it leaves you in that state of raucous domesticity, 'in with a shout'.

SCHRÖDINGER.
Yes. If only our other questions could remain unresolved a little while. Looking at these implausibility levels, provided the tank were to remain a secret, I feel Ireland could well stay neutral for, oh, as much as another year or two.

MYLES.
Ah, well, I suppose that was too much to hope for. Well, Erwin, it's been nice working with you. We had a good stab at it, dodging the inevitable with improbable frequency. But now . . .

Song: **UNRESOLVED** – *hesitant, questing.*

TRISTRAM *and* PHILOMENA.
Probabilities hang in the air,
Unresolved.
If I reach out, will you still be there –
Unresolved?

Do we wind up our song on a minor chord?
The lyrics in search of that final word –
Unresolved?

SCHRÖDINGER *and* MYLES.
So many questions remain
Unresolved.
Recurring again and again –
Unresolved,
Like particle-wave duality,
And the future of Irish neutrality –
Unresolved.

BETJEMAN *and* MYLES.
Our neighbourly rancour goes on,
Unresolved.
Much like it's been all along,
Unresolved.
We see in each other our own baser traits,
And the mutual awkwardness escalates –
Unresolved.

TRISTRAM *and* PHILOMENA.
I want you, whatever may be
Unresolved.
I'll stay with you happily –
Unresolved.
So let's take a gamble on you and me,
Unlikely bedfellows eternally –
Unresolved.

They smile at each other and move towards the bar.

Song: **WE'RE ALL IN THE GUTTER** (*reprise*).

ALL.
Well, things haven't worked out too badly –
Amazingly well, you might say.
A cynic might hint
That we're winning by dint
Of duplicitous, underhand play.
Well, here's what we say to the cynics,
As the vultures are circling around:
We're all in the gutter,
But some of us have an ear to the ground.

You'll find ample verification
In any half-decent book.

There's a verse in the Bible
That bears me right out,
Or I'm certain there is if you look.
Just remember this small piece of wisdom,
As simple as it is profound:
We're all in the gutter,
But some of us have an ear to the ground.

We're all in the gutter,
We're all in the gutter,
We're all in the gutter,
But some of us have an ear to the ground.

So we'll leave while the odds are still with us,
No wiser than when we began.
This wave of unlikelihood's all for the best,
So let's ride on the crest while we can.
But remember this lesson in physics,
Improbable as it may sound:
We're all in the gutter,
But some of us have an ear to the ground.

We're all in the gutter,
We're all in the gutter,
We're all in the gutter,
But some of us have an ear to the ground.

We're all in the gutter, etc.

Blackout.

The End.